Plants
(wildflowers)

Insects

Soil   Water

Insectivores

Decomposers
(Bacteria and Fungi)

wildflower
identifier

RICK IMES

Photographs provided by PHOTO/NATS, Boston

A QUINTET BOOK

An imprint of BDD Promotional Book
Company, Inc.
666 Fifth Avenue
New York, N.Y. 10103

Mallard Press and its accompanying design and logo
are trademarks of BDD Promotional Book
Company, Inc.

First published in the United States of America
in 1990 by The Mallard Press

ISBN 0-792-45348-4

This book was designed and produced by
Quintet Publishing Limited
6 Blundell Street
London N7 9BH

Creative Director: Peter Bridgewater
Designer: Dave Johnson
Project Editor: Caroline Beattie
Editor: Ann Ronan
Illustrators: Scott Weidensaul and Lorraine Harrison

Typeset in Great Britain by
Central Southern Typesetters, Eastbourne
Manufactured in Hong Kong by
Regent Publishing Services Limited
Printed in Hong Kong by
Leefung-Asco Printers Limited

MAIN COVER

COVER INSERTS

**Wildflower meadow in
Soldotna, Kenai
Peninsula, Alaska.**

1. Cardinal flower,
Lobelia cardinalis.

2. Painted trillium,
Trillium undulatum.

3. Blue columbine,
Aquilegia coerulea.

ACKNOWLEDGEMENTS

To Sandy, Krista, Samantha, and Hickory, for their encouragement,
support and patience. Without their sacrifices, this book could not have
been written.

wildflower
identifier

CONTENTS

INTRODUCTION
About Wildflowers

WHAT IS A WILDFLOWER?

As the name implies, wildflowers are flowering plants that grow wild; that is, they are able to reproduce without human intervention from seeds developed in the ovary of the flower.

Prairie, once one of the most abundant habitat types in North America, is quite diminished today. The chief culprit: agriculture.

Meadow habitat supports species, many of which are aliens, requiring long periods of direct sunlight.

Wildflowers are not necessarily native to the areas in which they are found. As a group, wildflowers include the so-called 'weeds' of lawns, gardens, roadsides, and disturbed soil, which were introduced accidentally or purposely from Europe or Asia. Native wildflowers, by contrast, evolved in North America in the very habitats where they are found today. They have only been associated with civilization for two or three hundred years, and most had not been confronted with widespread development until the past century. This is an extremely short time period for evolutionary adaptations to have occurred; consequently, native species do not compete well at all in developed areas. All of the rare and endangered wildflower species in this country are native, and the primary threat to their existence is habitat loss.

Trees, though flowering plants, are not considered wildflowers, and are generally distinguished by their size and by their woody stems which do not whither and die each year as do the fleshy, herbaceous stems of most temperate-zone wildflowers. There is debate among naturalists as to whether or not wild shrubs and vines should be considered "wildflowers". Though their stems are woody and they share many other characteristics with trees, some of the more common wild shrubs and vines have been included in this book because of their showy blooms.

Coniferous forests, like those blanketing much of the northern Rocky Mountains, favor shade-tolerant wildflower species. In the background is Long's Peak, Rocky Mountain National Park, Colorado.

THE ANATOMY OF WILDFLOWERS

Although there is considerable variation from one species to another, flowering plants can usually be divided into four major parts: leaves, roots, stem, and flower(s). Each part has different primary functions.

Leaves are the solar collector panels which power the plant. Though any green part of the plant can undergo photosynthesis, leaves are the main sites of photosynthetic production. Photosynthesis is a process in which the plant utilizes a green pigment, known as chlorophyll, to harness the energy of light and with it combine molecules of carbon dioxide from the air with water molecules to form simple sugars, called carbohydrates, with the release of oxygen. These carbohydrates fuel the plant, allowing it to carry out its functions of growth and reproduction.

Leaves are usually arranged on the stem so as to take maximum advantage of available sunlight, particularly in the more northern regions. This generally means that the largest leaves grow closest to the ground, sometimes in an arrangement called a basal rosette, and that the leaves grow progressively smaller up the stem. They are usually positioned so that they are not directly underneath each other. This arrangement shades the soil and helps to prevent it from overheating, and also discourages competing plants from growing too close.

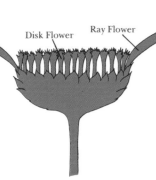

Disk Flower — Ray Flower

FLOWER PARTS

Disk

Rays

Involucre of bracts

PARTS OF A FLOWER

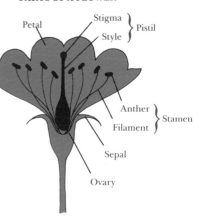

Petal — Stigma — Style } Pistil

Anther — Filament } Stamen

Sepal

Ovary

Simple Generic Flower

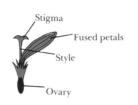

Stigma

Fused petals

Style

Ovary

Ray Flower

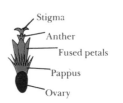

Stigma

Anther

Fused petals

Pappus

Ovary

Tubular Disk Flower

Another function of leaves is respiration, the exchange of gases involved in photosynthesis. On the undersides of leaves are tiny openings, called stomata, through which carbon dioxide enters and the by-products of photosynthesis, oxygen and water vapor, leave. Stomata open during daylight hours, when the need for carbon dioxide is greatest, and close at night. Although opening during the warmest hours of the day also accelerates water loss, the root system is normally able to maintain a sufficient supply to overcome this disadvantage.

The root system anchors the plant and extracts water and essential minerals from the soil, and transports them upward into the stem. It also helps to hold in place the thin layer of topsoil upon which it and most other plants depend. Two major types of root systems exist. Taproots are large and fleshy, and often reach deep into the ground. They are rather starchy and function as food storage sites during the dormant period of perennial plants. Fibrous root systems depend on branching filaments growing close to the soil's surface to collect precipitation before it sinks deeper into the ground. Many plants have combined these two root systems.

Stems serve as support for the leaves and flowers, positioning them where they can best accomplish their respective tasks. Additionally, the stems and roots house a vascular system of xylem and phloem, tube-like structures which conduct water and nutrients to various parts of the plant. Xylem transports water and dissolved substances upward in the plant. Phloem differs in that it can move materials up and down. It primarily transports newly-photosynthesized organic molecules, such as amino acids and carbohydrates, from the leaves to the roots and stem for storage or to the growing parts of the plant for immediate use.

Flowers are strictly reproductive structures. Their frequently showy appearance, distinctive fragrance, or both, attract the attention of potential pollinators, usually insects. Ultraviolet light is invisible to us, but not to insects; most insects cannot see deep red. Consequently, few flowers are deep red, but many reflect ultraviolet light. Deep red blooms have developed other means to attract pollinators; purple trillium, for instance, has also earned the name stinking Benjamin for the fetid odor it emits to attract carrion flies, its primary pollinators. Other flowers, some of which are too small to be seen, are wind-pollinated.

SCIENTIFIC AND COMMON NAMES

Naming a plant is not so simple as it might seem. Common names are generally used in everyday conversation, but some plants have more than one common name, while the same common name may be applied to distinctly different species. Trout lily, for example, is also known as dogtooth violet, yellow adder's tongue, and fawn lily. With over 350,000 species of plants known and many more yet to be discovered and classified, a precise system of classification and naming is essential.

The system of classifying and naming organisms in use by scientists around the world is a classification hierarchy, a series of categories arranged in order from general to specific relationships. In order of increasing specificity they are: kingdom, phylum, class, order, family, genus, and species. Each of these is a collective unit composed of one or more groups from the next higher category. A genus is a closely related group of species, a family is a closely related group of genera, and so on.

Eighteenth-century Swedish naturalist Carolus Linnaeus, affectionately known as the father of modern botany, introduced in 1753 a two-word system of naming organisms. This replaced the cumbersome method of a generic name followed by a long sequence of descriptive phrases that grew each time another member of that genus was discovered. The system invented by Linnaeus identifies each species with just two words: the first is the name of the genus to which that species belongs, while the second, frequently an adjective, designates the particular species of that genus. All scientific names are in Latin, although some have descriptive Greek roots. The name of the genus is always capitalized while the species name never is, and both are either underlined or printed in italics. When more than one member of the same genus is being discussed, the first word may be abbreviated, such as *C. acaule* for *Cypripedium acaule*.

Despite the simplicity and precision of Linnaeus' system, this book was written for the layperson whose Latin may be a little rusty, and therefore it has been organized alphabetically by common names.

Alien species do particularly well in disturbed or waste soils, conditions common to their native lands. Roadsides, railroad beds, strip mines, quarries, and construction sites all fall into this category. Butterfly weed (*Asclepias tuberosa*) is often found in such places.

***Gentiana crinita*, an eastern species shown here, and a western species, *Gentiana detonsa*, share the same common name, fringed gentian. Instances like this reinforce the need for the system of classification used in the scientific community.**

A WORLD OF WILDFLOWERS

No matter where you travel on Earth, it is difficult to find a place where wildflowers will not grow. With the exception of oceans and of fresh water bodies that are more than a few feet deep, these plants are truly worldwide, adapted to nearly every conceivable environment. We usually think of wildflowers as growing in meadows and forests, but you will also find them in marshes and shallow water, high above the timberline on mountains, and in deserts. Not only are wildflowers astonishingly widespread, but they are also incredibly diverse. While thousands of species are known to us, many more remain undiscovered and unclassified in more remote regions. It is small wonder that there are so many, really, for every part of a wildflower is subject to variation in form and function, making for endless combinations of features. To comprehend this fully, you must first understand the basics of evolution.

Evolution is the adaptation of organisms to their environment over countless generations. Although it was first proposed as a theory by nineteenth-century British naturalist Charles Darwin in his book, *The Origin of Species*, the available evidence overwhelmingly supports evolution, and it is accepted as fact by nearly all scientists. Natural selection is the mechanism by which evolution occurs. All living organisms are subject to random genetic mutations which manifest themselves through differences in the appearance, behavior, or capabilities of that organism's offspring. Most mutations have little or no effect on an organism's survival ability but there are possible mutations in any living thing that would impart a distinct advantage or disadvantage in the struggle to survive, and these are the key to the process of natural selection.

Consider an animal whose main defense against predators is to freeze so that its coloration camouflages it against a similar background. If its coloration gene mutated to produce an albino offspring, that animal would stand very little chance of surviving until sexual maturity when it could pass on the mutant gene to future generations. Conversely, a mutation that provides an edge over competing members of the same species in their struggle for survival means that the individual is more likely to attain sexual maturity, reproduce, and impart the same advantage to its progeny, who will go on to out-compete the other members of their generation, and so on, until, after an enormously long time period, the mutant gene finally displaces the "normal" gene within that species. In this way, ever so gradually, a species changes to the point where it becomes a separate species from its distant ancestors.

This is exactly the way our present diversity of flowering plants originated. Rolling the genetic dice determined which individuals and which species would be able to meet the demands of a constantly changing environment; the rest were simply eliminated.

WILDFLOWERS IN AN ECOSYSTEM

One of the most basic lessons of ecology is called the Web of Life. A spider's web serves as a model to illustrate the intertwined relationships of all living things with each other and with the non-living components of their environment, such as water, air, soil, and the sun.

Each point where the strands of the web intersect or attach represents an animal, plant, microorganism, or non-living factor. The strands themselves represent the relationships between all of these parts. Anyone who has ever toyed with the web of a spider knows that, while the intact web is a very strong structure indeed, it weakens with each strand that is disturbed until, at one critical point, the entire web collapses. So it is with the web of life.

Wildflowers are an integral part of our web. In reality, each species is represented by an individual point on the web, but such a complex model would be impossible to illustrate in this book. Instead, all wildflowers are represented by a single point on our illustration.

All parts and functions of a wildflower link it to the web of life. The plant as a whole absorbs carbon dioxide, one of the primary gases implicated in the ominous greenhouse effect occurring in the Earth's atmosphere, and replaces it with oxygen, which nearly all living things need to survive. It also, along with all other green plants, forms the base of all food chains on Earth by harnessing the sun's energy and converting it into chemical energy through photosynthesis, combining carbon dioxide and water to form simple sugars. These organic molecules feed not only the plant, but also all of the animals that graze upon it.

A spider's web is used to symbolize the "Web of Life," a powerful ecological concept. The strands represent relationships between different living and non-living segments of our environment, including ourselves. This model illustrates that we cannot disturb a portion of the web without altering the rest of it.

The highland desert of central Wyoming is an arid area of temperature extremes to which a surprising number of plants have adapted.

Shallow aquatic habitats such as slow-moving Myakka River in Florida often support a profusion of rooted, flowering plants. Shown here is water hyacinth, *Eichornia crassipes*.

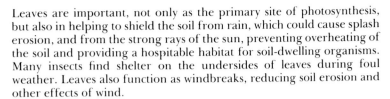

Alpine tundra is a land of stunted miniatures. Plants must grow close to the ground in order to avoid the force and dessication of high mountain winds.

Leaves are important, not only as the primary site of photosynthesis, but also in helping to shield the soil from rain, which could cause splash erosion, and from the strong rays of the sun, preventing overheating of the soil and providing a hospitable habitat for soil-dwelling organisms. Many insects find shelter on the undersides of leaves during foul weather. Leaves also function as windbreaks, reducing soil erosion and other effects of wind.

Flowers are the site of reproduction in most wildflowers, and thus are linked to other parts of the web by this fact alone. They also provide nectar and pollen to feed the insects which pollinate them, thereby feeding the insect-eaters of the world. Insects are the second-largest terrestrial food base, following green plants, so whatever feeds them is important indeed. Delightful, jewel-like hummingbirds and their close relatives also derive much of their nourishment from flowers while pollinating them in return.

Even the roots and stem can be individually linked in the web of life. They anchor and support the plant, making all of its other functions possible. Roots also hold in place the delicate layer of topsoil upon which most higher plants depend for water, minerals, and growing sites. Additionally, they help to aerate the soil, supplying air to the myriad of soil-dwelling creatures that condition the soil, improving it for plant growth.

Following their deaths, wildflowers continue to be linked to the web. Their tissue is decomposed by bacteria and fungi, nature's recyclers, who feed themselves while returning minerals and organic matter, called humus, to the soil, to the benefit of future generations of plants.

These are but a few examples of the multitude of roles wildflowers play in our environment. Our appreciation of their beauty is merely one of the fringe benefits of our own position within the web of life.

RARE AND ENDANGERED WILDFLOWERS

Rare and endangered animals have received a great deal of attention in the last two decades as our environmental awareness has grown. Most of us know of the plight of whales, California condors, whooping cranes, and other wildlife in today's headlines, but far fewer understand that many plants are also threatened with extinction. The common threat to endangered animals and plants alike is pressure exerted by human civilization, specifically in the form of habitat loss. Profound environmental changes in the United States within the last century have accelerated habitat loss to crisis proportions. Foremost among these changes have been the settling of the West and the increases in agricultural land and urban sprawl that accompany a booming human population.

Widespread agriculture and urbanization are the two dominant forces which have radically altered the North American landscape, to the detriment of many native wildflower species.

Habitat is the native environment of a plant or animal; it is a place or region that meets all of an organism's needs for survival. Your house is your habitat. If you live in the temperate or subarctic regions of the world and lose your house, you become endangered. Before the arrival of winter, you must find another suitable habitat, or else develop adaptations to protect yourself and your resources. Otherwise you face the probability of becoming extinct as an individual. This simplified analogy is appropriate to the situation faced by endangered wildlife. However, while we can still find vacant building sites on which to construct another home, wildlife habitat is a finite resource. Furthermore, the habitat still remaining already supports the maximum number of each species native to it; there is simply nowhere for displaced plants and animals to go.

Botanical gardens and wildflower preserves may slow the rate of plant extinction, but their capacity in this respect is limited. While they are wonderful places to visit, they are but islands in an expanding sea of human development that prevents their interaction with the rest of the ecosystem. Once a rare species is relegated to refuges such as this, it is as good as gone. This is much like taking a strand from the spider's web and hanging it elsewhere, for while it still exists, it has lost its function.

Extinction is final. Once a plant or animal becomes extinct, there will never be another of that species. With such a marvelous diversity of life on Earth, some may wonder if the loss of a wildflower species here or there is really significant. You can be certain that it is. Many of the so-called miracle drugs that have vastly improved our quality of life have been derived from plants. Who is to say that the showy lady's slipper does not hold a cure for AIDS, or that a derivative of trailing arbutus may not someday wipe out cancer?

One of the casualties of the disappearing prairie is the prairie white fringed orchid, *Habenaria leucophaea*, now listed as endangered by the federal government of the United States.

A good wildflower field guide covering most of the species in your region is essential for making positive identifications.

A common misconception of our day is that we have already discovered everything there is to discover, and that it is time to turn from exploration to exploitation. This could not be more wrong. The grand reality is that most discoveries are still waiting to be made. The tragedy of extinction is that we will never know what we have lost.

For a dramatic example of the significance of a species, mentally transport yourself back through time, millions of years ago, to the Mesozoic Era. Look around you. The vegetation covering the landscape is lush and strange. There are no birds, and dinosaurs are the dominant life forms. Those small, timid creatures you see scurrying for cover are mammals, the distant ancestors·of those with which you are familiar, including yourself. Comfort yourself with the knowledge that mass extinctions will wipe out most of the dinosaur species within a short period of time, allowing mammals to flourish and evolve into their twentieth-century forms. But what if that unknown catastrophe decimates mammals instead of dinosaurs? Anxiously, you rush back to the future and find with great relief that everything has occurred just as it should have. Now, however, you will always wonder, "What if it hadn't? What sort of a world might exist today . . . ?"

LOOKING AT WILDFLOWERS

After your disconcerting time voyage, you can now appreciate the value of each species, and this in turn should help you appreciate its beauty as well. You need only take time to examine a wildflower and it will bombard your faculties with sensations. Admire the brilliant scarlet hue of a cardinal flower. Savor the wonderful fragrance of violets and mints. Relish the velvety-soft texture of the leaves of common mullein. Every wildflower has its own unique combination of color, form, taste, texture, and fragrance.

A hand lens is a valuable tool: Intricate structures will jump out at you, revealing their details and perhaps their function as well. In some species, such as those in the buckwheat family, the single flower is so small that a hand lens is necessary to examine it. The only reason these flowers catch your attention is that they are borne in relatively large clusters on the plant. Quality hand lenses are available from biological supply companies and in the gift shops of many nature centers and natural history museums.

WILDFLOWER PHOTOGRAPHY

Wildflowers are nearly ideal natural subjects; they are beautiful, plentiful, and they cannot run or fly away. Even with such a cooperative subject, there can be problems such as wind and depth-of- field.

This photograph illustrates well the concept of depth-of-field. Notice that the butterfly, the dried flower head upon which it is perched, and the flower on the right are all in sharp focus, while the flower on the left, which is closer to the camera lens, and the leaves in the background are out of focus. The zone of sharp focus is referred to as depth-of-field.

To understand depth-of-field, you must first understand a basic principle of photography: A photograph records light. In order to be properly exposed, the correct amount of light must reach the film. This is a function of shutter speed and the size of the lens opening, called the aperture. It is much like filling a bucket exactly to the top with water from a faucet. A slow trickle will take longer to fill the bucket than opening the faucet all the way. With too much water, the bucket overflows; too little and it is not full. Similarly, proper exposure of a photograph requires a longer shutter speed when using a small aperture than when using a larger one. Too much light results in overexposure; too little produces underexposure.

Once they catch the photography bug, some people really immerse themselves in it! This devotee is photographing bog plants in New Hampshire.

Depth-of-field is the area within a certain range of distances from the camera lens which is in focus. Anything in front of or behind this range will be out of focus. Depth-of-field is determined by the size of the aperture. A smaller aperture yields a greater depth-of-field than a larger aperture, and consequently will result in more of the plant being in focus. Using smaller apertures requires longer shutter speeds, which brings us to our next problem, wind. (It should also be noted that longer shutter speeds require the use of a tripod.)

The stems of most wildflower species are flexible, and the slightest breeze can set them swaying, resulting in blurred photographs when a slow shutter speed is used. The only strategies to counter this are to use either a fast shutter speed, which reduces the depth-of-field, a flash, or a wind screen. An excellent wind screen is a lean-to constructed from translucent sheets of plastic, such as those used to cover flourescent lights. Not only will it block moderate breezes, but it eliminates harsh shadows produced by direct sunlight.

GROWING WILDFLOWERS

Gardening is the most popular hobby in the United States, with a current trend toward natural landscaping and wildflower gardening. There are many reasons for this interest in native plants.

Native plants, which are well adapted to life in that particular region, require little or no pruning, trimming, watering, or fertilizing. Little weeding is necessary because those plants commonly known as "weeds" are usually wildflowers common to the area. Yearly planting of flowerbeds can be eliminated or cut back by selecting perennial species. Most attractive of all, the increased use of native plants means a reduction in lawn area, which is very expensive to maintain in terms of time, fertilizer, herbicide, water, and fossil fuel consumption. The beauty of the natural landscaping concept is that, in addition to all of the advantages mentioned, it can actually increase the value of your home. A well-planned landscape design utilizing native plants will make even the plainest of houses appear custom-built, assuming that they are well maintained otherwise.

Wildflower gardens can have one of many themes, or, with larger lots, several different themes can be used. It is best to examine the existing conditions on your land and the natural communities in the surrounding areas, then choose your theme accordingly. A landowner in Vermont would have as little success in establishing a cactus garden as the homeowner who tried to create a water garden in Arizona, and both would look quite out of place even if they were successful. One popular trend is the incorporation of water, shelter, and food sources for wildlife into natural landscapes, in effect creating a backyard wildlife refuge. By doing this, you can enjoy the activities of wild creatures around your home while helping to counter the effects of urban sprawl which threatens them. Several excellent volumes dealing with wildflower gardening and backyard wildlife habitats are listed in the appendix of this book.

Thoughtful selection of species to be included in your wild garden will yield benefits beyond the beauty of the plants themselves. The inclusion of food sources, like riverbank grape (*Vitis riparia*) shown here, will provide many hours of enjoyment through the wildlife they attract.

WILDFLOWER FOLKLORE

Wildflower literature is rich with folklore and legends extolling the origins and powers of various species. Some of these date back to the ancient Greeks and Romans, who were fond of explaining the universe in terms of the whims and wills of their gods. Others arose from northern European cultures, and quite a few have been handed down over the centuries by Native Americans. Many are of unknown origin.

It would seem that nearly every predicament faced by humankind prior to the Industrial Revolution could be corrected using one species of wildflower or another. There were plants that could be used to cast or lift spells, bring about love or marriage between two people, repel evil spirits, ease labor during childbirth, bestow good fortune, and so on. Plants, including wildflowers, met a great deal of the physical needs of our ancestors, including food, dyes, tools, utensils, shelter, and medicine. In earlier times, there were often few doctors and no pharmacists to visit when illness or injury struck. The people of those times lived much closer to nature than we do today, and used plants to treat or cure nearly every ailment. Those who professed expertise in these areas were known as herbalists, and many treatments prescribed by them were quite effective. This should not surprise us; a large percentage of the drugs used in modern medicine are from plants.

The language of Jack-in-the-pulpit (*Arisaema atrorubens*) is ardor and zeal, just the message a lover would wish to convey to his or her beloved.

Still, there were some false assumptions made with regard to the powers of plants. One of the most notable of these was the doctrine of signatures, a theory proposed by a Swiss physician in 1657. It declared that some plants had "signatures" which identified them as useful medicines, and that one had only to interpret these signatures correctly in order to find the cure for a given ailment. In reality, most of the treatments precribed under the doctrine of signatures were ineffective, and some may have been quite harmful to the patient. The legacies of this theory are the names given to the plants it prescribed, many of which persist to this day.

An elaborate language of flowers was developed during the 1700s and grew to be a popular form of communication. For instance, the language of the dandelion is "faithful to you," and it was sent in order to reassure an uncertain lover. This language grew to be so extensive that several dictionaries were written to explain the meaning of different species. In the days when many citizens were illiterate, this was actually a very practical means of communicating over distance.

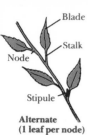

Blade
Stalk
Node
Stipule

Alternate
(1 leaf per node)

Arrow-head shaped

Basal

Banner
Wing
Keel

Pea Family Flower

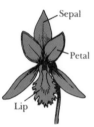

Sepal
Petal
Lip

Orchid Family Flower

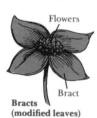

Flowers
Bract

Bracts
(modified leaves)

Clasping

GLOSSARY

alien
A species introduced from a different geographical area.
alpine
The region which lies above the treeline on mountains.
alternate leaves
Leaves which grow singly from each point on different sides of the stem.
annual
A plant which completes its life cycle in one growing season.
anther
The pollen-bearing portion of the stamen.
aquatic
A plant that grows in water.
arrowhead-shaped
Refers to the pointed shape of a leaf with two pointed lobes extending backward from the place of the leaf stalk's attachment.
axil
The upper angle formed where the leaf joins the stem.

banner
The uppermost petal of a pea flower.
basal leaves
Leaves that grow from the base of the plant stem.
bearded
Fringed or hairy, usually refering to the petals.
biennial
A plant that requires two years to complete its life cycle, only flowering in the second growing season.
bilateral symmetry
A flower shape which can be divided in half by only one line, also called irregular.
blade
The flat part of a leaf, sepal, or petal.
bog
An acidic, aquatic environment formed by a water-filled glacial depression, typically covered at least partially by a floating mat of vegetation.
bracts
Small, modified leaf-like structures often found at the base of a flower or floral cluster.
bulb
A swollen, underground portion of the stem functioning as food storage.

calyx
The collective term for the sepals of a flower.
carnivorous
An organism which derives its nutrition from the digestion of animal tissue.
clasping
A descriptive term for a leaf whose base curls up to partly or entirely surround the stem.
column
The structure of an orchid flower formed by the united stamens, style, and stigma.
compound leaf
A single leaf divided into smaller leaflets.
coniferous
Cone-bearing trees such as pine or spruce.
corolla
The collective term for the petals of a flower.
corymb
A flat-topped, branched flower cluster in which the branches alternate.
creeper
A trailing or prostrate stem, rooting as it goes to form a new plant.
cross-pollination
The transfer of pollen from one plant to another which ensures genetic diversity.
cyme
A flat-topped, branched flower cluster in which the branches are opposite.

deciduous
A plant that sheds its leaves and enters a dormant period at the end of each growing season.
disk flower
The small tubular flowers in the central disk of the flower heads in some members of the composite family.

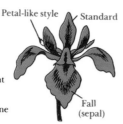

Petal-like style — Standard

Fall
(sepal)

Iris Family Flower

HABITAT SYMBOLS

DECIDUOUS FOREST

OPEN WOODS

CONIFEROUS FOREST

FOREST EDGE

THICKET/BRUSH/
SAGEBRUSH

GRASSLAND/PRAIRIE

MEADOW/PASTURE/
OLD FIELDS

ROADSIDES/WASTE AREA/
DISTURBED SOIL

Corymb

Finely Dissected,
fern-like

Entire

dissected leaves
Deeply cut leaves in which the division does not reach to the midrib.
divided leaves
The same as dissected leaves.
downy
Densely covered with fine hairs.

elliptical
Widest in the middle and tapering equally toward both ends.
emergent
Aquatic plants whose stems and leaves extend significantly above the water's surface.
entire
A smooth leaf margin with no teeth, lobes, or divisions.
egg-shaped
Broader near one end and tapering toward the other, one and one-half to two times longer than wide.

fall
One of the sepals of an iris flower.
filament
The anther-bearing stalk of a stamen.
fruit
The fertilized, ripened ovary of a flower.
fused
United or joined so that the separate parts are not easily distinguished.

genera
Plural of genus, a group of closely related species.
glandular
Bearing glands which secrete oil or nectar.

head
A crowded cluster of short-stalked or stalkless flowers.
herbaceous
Soft or succulent; not woody.

inflorescence
A flower cluster.
introduced
Not native to the particular region being discussed.
involucre
A collective term for a whorl of bracts beneath a flower or a flower cluster.
irregular flower
A flower with bilateral symmetry, in which the shape can be divided in half by only one possible line.

keel
The two lower petals of a pea flower united to resemble the bottom of a boat.

lance-shaped
Broadest near one end and tapering toward the other, several times longer than wide.
lateral
Located on the sides.
leaflet
One of the leaf-like segments of a compound leaf.
linear
Long, narrow, and tapering with entire margins; grass-like.
lip petal
The lower, often showy petal of some irregular flowers such as orchids.
lobed
Rounded indentations in the leaf margin not reaching to the midrib.

margin
The edge of a leaf, leaflet, or petal.
midrib
The central vein of a leaf or leaflet.

native
Having originated in the region being discussed.
node
The point of attachment of leaves and branches to the stem.

oblong
Longer than broad with parallel sides and rounded ends.
opposite leaves
Paired leaves attached to the stem at the same point but on opposite sides.

Elliptical

Egg-shaped

Heart-shaped

Head

Irregular
(bilaterally
symmetrical)

Spathe
Spadix

Arum Family
Flower

Linear

Lance-shaped

Pinnately lobed

Lobed

Oblong

oval
Broadly elliptical; widest in the middle and tapering quickly to both ends.
ovary
The enlarged base of the pistil in which eggs are housed and seeds develop.

palmate leaves
Leaves having three or more segments, lobes, or leaflets radiating outward from the base, as fingers radiate outward from one's palm.
panicle
An elongated, alternately branched flower cluster.
perennial
A plant that normally lives more than two years, growing back from the rootstock after each dormant period.
perianth
The combined calyx and corolla.
petal
One segment of the corolla, usually flat, broad, and brightly colored.
petiole
The stalk of a leaf.
photosynthesis
The process by which green plants use sunlight to convert carbon dioxide (taken from the air) into simple carbohydrates (with the release of oxygen).
pinnate leaves
Leaves in which the segments, lobes, or leaflets are arranged down the sides of a central stalk or midrib, much like the pinnae, or hair-like structures, of a feather.
pistil
The female organ of a flower, composed of the ovary, style, and stigma.
pollen
The male spores produced by the anther.
pollination
The transfer of pollen from an anther to a stigma.
prairie
One of several types of grassland habitat in midwestern North America.
prostrate
Creeping or trailing; lying flat on the ground.

raceme
An elongated flower cluster in which short-stalked flowers bloom along a common stem.
radial symmetry
Wheel-shaped flowers which can be divided in half by an infinite number of lines; also called regular.
ray flower
Bilaterally symmetrical flowers resembling a single petal on the floral head in members of the composite family.
recurved
Curved first one way and then the opposite way.
reflexed
Bent strongly backward.
regular flower
A wheel-shaped flower having radial symmetry.
rhizome
A horizontal underground stem, often elarged for food storage.
rosette
A crowded cluster of leaves encircling the base of the stem.
runner
A creeping or trailing stem, often taking root and developing a new plant at its tip.

saprophyte
A non-green plant which derives its nourishment from dead organic matter.
sepal
A single segment of the calyx which is usually green, but sometimes is colored differently and strongly resembles a petal.
shrub
A low, woody plant with several or many woody stems originating at the base of the plant.
simple leaf
A leaf not divided into leaflets.
spadix
A dense spike of miniscule flowers formed by members of the arum family.

**Opposite
(2 leaves
per node)**

— Node

Oval

Leaflet

Palmate

Panicle

Leaflet

Twice-pinnate

Leaflet

Once-pinnate

Raceme

**WETLANDS/SHORELINE/
STREAM BANK**

BOGS

DESERT

ALPINE – MOUNTAIN

MOUNTAINS

AQUATIC

MOIST

DRY

**ROCKY SLOPES/CLIFF/
OUTCROP**

BLOOMING PERIOD SYMBOL

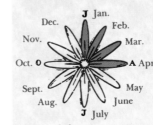

Shaded rays represent approximate blooming period.

spathe
A large, sheath-like bract or pair of bracts encircling the spadix in members of the arum family.
species
The narrowest group of organisms sharing common characteristics. Each species is denoted by a two-word Latin name.
spike
An elongated flower cluster with stalkless flowers growing along a common stem.
spur
A slender, hollow projection from part of a flower.
stamen
The male organ of a flower composed of a filament and an anther.
standard
One of the petals of an iris flower.
stigma
The tip of the pistil, often sticky, which receives pollen.
style
The stalk of the pistil which connects the ovary and the stigma.
succulent
Thick, fleshy, water-storing stems or leaves.

taproot
A large, vertical main root from which smaller rootlets emerge.
tendril
A slender, coiling structure which anchors climbing plants.
terminal
At the end of a stem or branch.
toothed
A saw-like edge.
tuber
A short, thick underground stem serving as food storage.

umbel
A flower cluster, often flat or slightly convex, in which all of the flower stalks originate from a common point.
undulating
Wavy.

whorled
Three or more leaves, bracts, or flowers radiating from a single point on the stem.
wing
The two lateral petals of a pea flower.

**Regular
(radially
symmetrical)**

Basal Rosette

Spike

**Solitary
terminal**

**Finely
toothed**

**Coarsely
toothed**

Umbel

PLANT HEIGHT

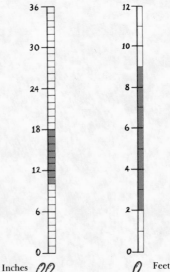

36	12
30	10
24	8
18	6
12	4
6	2
0	0

Inches   Feet

Shaded area represents range of height for mature plant.

Node

**Whorled
(3 or more
leaves per node)**

IDENTIFYING WILDFLOWERS

WILDFLOWER FAMILIES

Families are handy units with which to begin your study of wildflowers. A family is large enough to include species with general similarities, yet small enough so as not to be too cumbersome.

Studying family characteristics and wildflower structures makes wildflower identification much easier and faster by narrowing the possibilities from many thousands to a relatively small handful. If you are out in the field without a wildflower guide, knowing the family traits will often allow you to limit the prospects enough to make a firm identification of your find with the help of a reference book once you get home. More than one hundred families of wildflowers exist in temperate North America, far more than is practical for us to cover in the scope of this book. This section contains a brief overview of the larger families covered later. If the remainder of this text stirs your interest in wildflowers as it is intended to, there are comprehensive field guides available for all geographic regions that will enable you to learn more.

Buttercup Family   Ranunculaceae

The buttercup family is somewhat variable. Flowers may be regular or irregular. Sepals and petals vary from 5 to many, and are separate. Occasionally, the petals are absent and the sepals appear petal-like. Stamens are usually numerous, with one or more pistils. The leaves are usually alternate and palmately lobed or divided, but may sometimes be opposite, pinnately lobed, or simple. This family has very diverse habitat requirements.

Daisy Family   Compositae

This is the largest family of wildflowers, and also the most evolutionarily advanced. The flowers are tightly packed into a floral head that allows many flowers to be pollinated by a single insect visit. Two types of flowers occur in the daisy family: ray flowers, irregular, with their 5 petals fused together in a flattened, strap-like corolla, and disk flowers, which are tubular and radially symmetrical. Each flower consists of a fused corolla, a column of stamens with fused anthers, and a pistil with a two-lobed stigma. Heads may consist of all disk flowers, all ray flowers, or a central group of disk flowers encircled by ray flowers. Below the head is a whorl of bracts called the involucre. Leaves may be simple or compound, and arranged alternately,

Lily family – trout lily, *Erythronium americanum.*

oppositely, or in a whorl. You will often find the daisy family in open habitats.

Heath Family   Ericaceae

Members of the heath family have long delighted the palettes of Americans, for they include the cranberries and blueberries. These are woody, shrubby plants favoring acidic bogs and mountain habitats. Flowers may be regular or irregular. Sepals number 4 or 5 and are fused. Four or five petals are also fused, often in the shape of a globe or Chinese lantern. Reproductive structures consist of 8 or 10 stamens and a single pistil. Leaves are simple, usually alternate, and frequently leathery.

Lily Family   Liliaceae

Larger members of the lily family, such as tulips, hyacinths, and tiger lilies, are favored by gardeners. The flowers of this family are either bell-shaped and nodding, cup-shaped and upright, or triangular. There are 3 sepals, which may strongly resemble petals, and 3 petals, usually free but sometimes united. The flower is completed by six stamens and one pistil terminating in a tri-lobed stigma. Leaves of the bulbed perennials are parallel-veined, long, blade-like, and basal. Those of the other species are simple and either alternate or whorled. Some of these are woodland wildflowers, while others prefer thickets, meadows, and forest clearings.

Mint Family — Labiatae

The mints are among the most aromatic of wildflowers, particularly when their glandular foliage is crushed. they are characterized by their *square* stems, which few species outside of this family possess. Their flowers are bilaterally symmetrical, with 5 united sepals and 5 petals fused to form two flared lips, the upper lip having two lobes and the lower one with three lobes. Each flower includes between 2 and 4 stamens and one pistil. Leaves are simple and either opposite or whorled. Mint flowers grow in short spikes or clustered in the leaf axils. Habitats in which you are likely to find mints are lawns, meadows, and forest clearings.

Mustard Family — Cruciferae

The mustard family includes many familiar vegetables, such as cabbages, radishes, and turnips, and is also the source of the familiar table condiment. The flowers have four separate petals arranged in a distinct cross-shape, hence the scientific name. They also possess four individual sepals, one pistil, and six stamens, the outer two usually being shorter than the others. Leaves are normally alternate and simple, but may be pinnately divided. Wildflowers of the mustard family typically prefer fields, meadows, and roadsides.

Orchid Family — Orchidaceae

If there were a crown jewel of wildflowers, it would surely be the orchid family. The configuration and color of their blooms lightens the heart of even the most pragmatic person. Orchids occupy diverse habitats from arctic tundra to tropical rainforest. Orchid flowers are bilaterally symmetrical and composed of three sepals, two lateral petals, and a third petal differing in form, color, and size. The odd petal is usually larger, sometimes forms a lip or pouch, and often has a spur. One or two stamens are fused with the pistil, forming a column at the flower's core. Orchid leaves have parallel veins and are basal or alternate.

Pea Family — Leguminosae

Legumes, as species in this family are known, include peas, beans, soybeans, peanuts, lentils, and clovers. The most typical flower is irregular with 5 petals; the lower two join to form a keel like that on a boat, the two lateral petals are called wings, and the broad upper petal is the banner. Ten stamens, nine of which are fused, are hidden within the keel. Leaves are commonly alternate and pinnately or palmately compound. Members of the pea family are valued by farmers for their economic worth and because they store

Rose family – rugosa rose, *Rosa rugosa*.

Orchid family – nodding ladies' tresses, *Spiranthes cernua*.

nitrogen in root nodules, thus enriching the soil in which they grow. These are plants of open habitats, particularly roadsides and fields.

Pink Family — Caryophyllaceae

At least one member of the pink family is familiar to everyone, that being the carnation sold in abundance by florists. Related wildflowers are not nearly as showy, however. Their blossoms consist of 5 sepals, 5 petals, 5 to 10 stamens, and a pistil. The petals are often slender at the base and fringed, toothed, or notched at the tip. Leaves of the pinks are simple and opposite. The *swollen nodes of the stems* distinguish pinks from nearly all other families except the buckwheat family, whose members have alternate leaves and inconspicuous flowers lacking petals. Pinks prefer open habitats.

Rose Family — Rosaceae

Garden-variety roses have been selectively bred to produce the blooms with which we are familiar. Their wild relatives are much simpler, and beautiful in their simplicity. Radially symmetric, they have 5 sepals, 5 round, separate petals, numerous stamens attached to the edge of a central cup-shaped structure, and one or many pistils. Leaves may be simple but are most often compound. As a group, they are quite diverse, occupying nearly every habitat type. Including such favorites as apples, cherries, peaches, pears, plums, raspberries, blackberries, and strawberries, the rose family is responsible for many of our most popular foods.

Snapdragon Family — Scrophulariaceae

Perky, brightly-colored snapdragons are beautiful flowers displaying bilateral symmetry. The calyx is composed of 4 or 5 united sepals, and 4 or 5 petals are fused to form a corolla with an upper and lower lip. Four stamens are ordinarily present with one pistil. The shape and arrangement of the leaves are variable from one species to another. The snapdragon family's assorted habitat preferences enable them to be very widespread. It is distinguished from the mint family by its round stems.

Violet Family — Violaceae

Equally at home in a forest, meadow, or lawn, violets have brightly colored blooms which are most often bilaterally symmetrical, with 5 separate sepals, 5 separate petals, 5 united stamens, and one pistil. The lower petal is often largest and functions as a sort of landing pad for pollinating insects. It has dark veins known as "bee guides" or "honey guides" which lead the insect to a backward-projecting, nectar-filled spur. On its way to the nectar, the insect fulfills its primary function of pollination. Violet leaves are alternate or basal; they are simple, but may be deeply lobed.

ARUM FAMILY — Araceae

JACK-IN-THE-PULPIT
Arisaema triphyllum

"Jack" is actually a club-shaped spadix bearing either male or female flowers, enveloped by the "pulpit", a canopy-forming spathe striped with green and purplish-brown. This is always accompanied by one or two basal leaves palmately divided into lanced-shaped leaflets with entire margins.

The sex of the flowers is determined by the amount of food stored in the corm during the last growing season. More energy is required to develop fruit to maturity than to produce pollen. Therefore, a plant will produce two leaves and female flowers only if it has stored a large quantity of food. If the amount of food stored is less than optimum, Jack-in-the-pulpit produces either one leaf and male flowers, or, under the poorest conditions, one leaf and no flowers, electing to merely survive.

Range: Quebec to New Brunswick, south to Florida and Texas.

ARUM FAMILY — Araceae

SKUNK CABBAGE
Symplocarpus foetidus

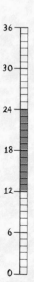

One whiff reveals the origin of both the common name and the specific name, *foetidus*, which means "evil smelling." The mild odor of decaying flesh, along with the purplish-red color of the shell-like spathe, attracts carrion flies which pollinate this early spring wildflower.

The spathe encloses a knobby, yellow spadix covered with minute, inconspicuous flowers. Through cellular respiration, the plant actually produces enough heat to melt snow around it and to keep the temperature inside the spadix at about 70°F intensifying the odor emanating it.

The dark green, basal leaves grow to 12-24 inches long and up to 12 inches wide and have an entire margin. They generally do not appear until after the flowers have bloomed.

Range: Southwestern Manitoba to Quebec, south to Georgia and Iowa.

COMMON BARBERRY
Berberis vulgaris

This thorny shrub is both a bane to farmers and a boon to wildlife. Common barberry is an intermediate host of the fungus that causes black stem rust in wheat. It also forms dense, tangled masses in old fields, pastures, and fencerows, but it is this very quality that makes it superb cover for wildlife. In addition, its bright orange berries are relished as a winter food source by many birds and small mammals.

Common barberry's yellow flowers are approximately ¼ inch wide with six sepals, six petals, and six stamens. They dangle in racemes from arching branches where oval, 1–3 inch long toothed leaves grow in clusters.

Range: Ontario to Nova Scotia, south to Delaware and Missouri.

MAYAPPLE
Podophyllum peltatum

The solitary, nodding flower of mayapple typically grows from the crotch between two palmately lobed, umbrella-like leaves. It has 6–9 waxy, white petals with two bright yellow stamens per petal. The leaves are deeply lobed, up to 12 inches across, shiny on their top surface, and coarsely toothed.

The common name refers to the May blooming of a flower which resembles an apple blossom. *Podophyllum peltatum* is derived from two Greek words meaning "shield-shaped leaf." Its leaves, roots, and seeds are poisonous in large quantities, but, despite this, Shawnee Indians used the boiled roots as a laxative. Appalachian folklore says that a woman who pulls up the root of a mayapple soon becomes pregnant. Check under "partridgeberry" (*see* page 16) in the bedstraw family if this should happen to you!

Range: Southern Ontario to Quebec, south to Florida and Texas.

BEDSTRAW FAMILY   Rubiaceae

PARTRIDGEBERRY
Mitchella repens

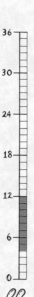

Partridgeberry's fragrant flowers grow in pairs of white or pink tubular blossoms, ½–¾ inch long, with four spreading lobes. Each pair is composed of one male and one female flower. The round, shiny, white-veined leaves are oppositely arranged and are about the same size as the flowers.

A trailing, evergreen plant, partridgeberry makes an excellent ground cover underneath acid-loving shrubs such as azaleas and rhododendrons. Its specific name, *repens*, means "creeping" or "trailing."

Cherokee Indian women made tea from this plant and drank it for several weeks before childbirth in the belief that it would speed the process and ease their labor.

Range: Ontario to Newfoundland, south to Georgia and Louisiana.

BEDSTRAW FAMILY   Rubiaceae

BLUETS
Houstonia caerulea

These cheerful, pale blue flowers often grow in large, dense masses that resemble patches of snow from a distance. Each flower is ½ inch wide, and is composed of four light blue petals fused together into a tubular corolla with spreading lobes and a golden center. The leaves basal or opposite and oblong, with entire margins.

The word *caerulea* means "sky blue" in Latin.

Range: Ontario to Nova Scotia, south to Georgia and Louisiana.

BLUEBELL FAMILY   Campanulaceae

CARDINAL FLOWER
Lobelia cardinalis

Cardinal flowers display perhaps the most brilliant red to be found in nature. They are a favorite of hummingbirds, which are their chief pollinators, as insects have a difficult time maneuvering inside the long corollas.

The bloom is bilaterally symmetrical and is composed of a 1½ inch long, two-lipped corolla. The upper lip has two lobes, while the lower, protruding lip is triple-lobed. Fused stamens form a tube around the style and project beyond the flower's opening. The alternate, lance-shaped leaves are toothed and may be from 2–6 inches long.

The common name of cardinal flower arose because of its similarity to the scarlet robes worn by Roman Catholic cardinals.

Range: California to Minnesota and new Brunswick, south to Florida and Texas.

BLUEBELL FAMILY   Campanulaceae

HAREBELL
Campanula rotundifolia

Harebell was once associated with witches, who were believed to transform themselves into hares, bestowing bad luck when they crossed a person's path.

The nodding, blue, bell-shaped flowers are either solitary or grow in loose clusters. They are less than one inch long, with a five-lobed corolla and five lavender-colored stamens. Stem leaves are alternate and entire, while basal leaves are broadly egg-shaped.

Range: Alaska to Labrador, south to New Jersey, Missouri, and Arizona.

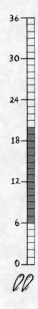

BUCKWHEAT FAMILY   Polygonaceae

CURLY DOCK
Rumex crispus

The reddish-green flowers grow in a branching raceme and possess six sepals but no petals. Each flower is less than ¼ inch long.

Curly dock seeds were used by American Indians to make flour. The leaves are also edible, with a bitter lemony flavor. Ounce for ounce, curly dock contains more vitamin C than orange juice and more vitamin A than carrots. It has been known since ancient times as a cure for "loose teeth," or scurvy, which results from a vitamin C deficiency.

Range: Throughout most of North America.

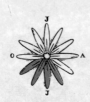

BUCKWHEAT FAMILY   Polygonaceae

LADY'S THUMB
Polygonum persicaria

The dark green triangle on each leaf may have been thought to resemble a lady's thumbprint, or perhaps the size and shape of the floral spike earned this wildflower its common name; however, its origin still remains uncertain.

Its pink flowers are borne in dense cylindrical spikes atop simple or branching stems. Each flower is less than ½ inch long and has from 4–6 sepals and no petals. The lance-shaped leaves are alternate and entire, with the afore-mentioned marking in the middle.

Range: Throughout most of North America.

BUCKWHEAT FAMILY — Polygonaceae

SULPHUR FLOWER
Eriogonum umbellatum

Sulphur flowers occur within a compound umbel (umbels arranged in an umbel) which forms a yellow or cream-colored ball-shaped cluster 2–4 inches in diameter. Their ½ inch flowers consist of six hairy sepals and nine stamens. Stem leaves are oval, very hairy underneath, and whorled at the ends of short, woody branches, while the spoon-shaped basal leaves are arranged in a rosette

The specific name, *umbellatum*, alludes to the structure of the flower cluster.

Range: British Columbia to Montana, south to Colorado and California.

BUTTERCUP FAMILY — Ranunculaceae

BLUE COLUMBINE
Aquilegia coerulea

The exquisite blue columbine is fittingly distinguished as Colorado's state flower. Its generic name, *aquilegia*, is derived from the Latin term for eagle, referring to the talon-like spurs of the blossom.

Five white, scoop-shaped petals project backward into nectar-filled spurs surrounded by five sky-blue sepals. Numerous stamens and five sepals protrude from the center of each upward-tipped flower. The compound, basal leaves are each divided into three deeply-lobed leaflets, giving the plant a bushy appearance.

Range: Western Montana to northern Arizona and northern New Mexico.

BUTTERCUP FAMILY   Ranunculaceae

CANADA ANEMONE
Anemone canadensis

Five white petal-like sepals of unequal size, along with numerous golden-yellow stamens and pistils, compose this showy representative of the buttercup family. Three stalkless, wedge-shaped leaves are whorled on the lower stem, while those on the upper stem are opposite. All are deeply lobed and toothed.

The roots of Canada anemone were used medicinally by Native Americans. It owes its common and specific names to its geographical distribution, which extends far into the northern reaches of Canada.

Range: Alberta to Maine, south to West Virginia and Colorado.

BUTTERCUP FAMILY   Ranunculaceae

PASQUE FLOWER
Anemone patens

Pasque flower is the state flower of South Dakota and is a true harbinger of spring on North America's prairies and tundra. The common name is derived from the French word for Easter and refers to the beginning of its blooming period. Pasque flower leaves contain a chemical that produces blisters, a property used by Blackfoot Indians as they bound the leaves over boils and sores to draw out infection.

The pasque flower blossom is about 2½ inches wide with 5–7 blue, purple, or white petal-like sepals (the petals are absent). The stamens are long and numerous, and there are many pistils as well. A silky-haired stem holds three whorled leaves with linear segments.

Range: Alaska to Ontario, south to Texas and New Mexico.

BUTTERCUP FAMILY   *Ranunculaceae*

SHARP-LOBED HEPATICA
Hepatica acutiloba

Basal, leathery leaves, approximately 2½ inches wide with three pointed lobes, are typical of this plant. The one-inch-wide flowers lack petals but have 5–9 sepals that may be pink, blue, or white. Its stem is hairy.

One of the earliest spring wildflowers in the eastern forests, sharp-lobed hepatica once indicated the time for spring planting. Since the shape of its leaf is like that of a liver, early herbalists used it to treat liver ailments. Its specific name means "sharp-lobed," a reference to its pointed leaves.

Range: Minnesota to Maine, south to Georgia, northern Alabama, and Missouri.

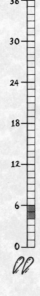

BUTTERCUP FAMILY   *Ranunculaceae*

SUBALPINE BUTTERCUP
Ranunculus escholtzii

Flowers on the subalpine buttercup are often so dense that they nearly obscure the foliage. They are about one inch wide with five shiny, brilliant yellow petals and numerous stamens. The leaves are generally about one inch long, round or egg-shaped, and they vary from having three shallow lobes to highly divided segments.

Like most alpine plants, subalpine buttercup grows close to the ground to protect itself from the harsh winds and freezing temperatures that are common at high elevations.

Range: Alaska to Alberta, south to Northern New Mexico and California.

BUTTERCUP FAMILY   Ranunculaceae

WILD COLUMBINE
Aquilegia canadensis

*A*quilegia, the Latin name for "eagle," refers to the red, talon-like spurs of this woodland beauty. These spurs are hollow and contain nectar sought by hummingbirds and bumblebees alike. Pollination occurs as the hovering hummingbird's belly rubs against the anthers and stigma, or as the bumblebees cling upside-down on the flower while trying to reach the nectar. Occasionally, a bee will take a shortcut and chew off the spurs to get at the nectar, in which case no pollination occurs.

Five upward-spurred, scoop-shaped petals are yellow on the blade and red on the spur. Numerous stamens hang below the drooping, bell-like flower which measures 1–2 inches in length. The calyx is composed of five red sepals. Alternate, long-stalked, and pinnately compound, the leaves have from 9–27 pale green, tri-lobed leaflets.

Range: Wisconsin to Maine, south to Georgia and Tennessee.

BUTTERCUP FAMILY   Ranunculaceae

TALL BUTTERCUP
Ranunculus acris

*F*ive glossy, yellow petals with waxy textures comprise the one-inch-wide corolla of tall buttercup. Both stamens and pistils are plentiful on these blooms. The foliage consists of both alternate and basal leaves, 1–4 inches wide and palmately divided into three lobes which are themselves divided.

This European introduction is well-adapted to compete with the tall meadow grasses common to its habitats. *Ranunculus* means "little frog," and is indicative of the moist habitats in which many members of this genus are found. *Acris* refers to the disagreeably bitter taste which discourages browsing by livestock.

Range: Throughout most of North America.

BUTTERCUP FAMILY   Ranunculaceae

WOOD ANEMONE
Anemone quinquefolia

There are 4–9 white sepals, along with numerous stamens and pistils, which comprise the inch-wide flower of wood anemone. There is a whorl of three leaves, each palmately divided into 3–5 toothed segments.

Wood anemone is named from Anemos, Greek god of the winds, and is also called "wind flower," because its slender stalks cause the flowers to quiver in the slightest breeze. They commonly grow in large stands on woodland borders.

Range: Quebec to Maine, south to North Carolina; also in Ohio and Kentucky.

CACTUS FAMILY   Cactaceae

PRICKLY PEAR
Opuntia humifusa

This is the only widespread eastern cactus. Its stem consists of flat, green, succulent pads, oblong or circular in shape, covered with clusters of short, reddish-brown bristles. Though lacking the dangerous spines of its western relatives, the barbed bristles of prickly pear are just as painful and more difficult to remove. The showy flowers are yellow, often with a reddish center, and consist of numerous sepals, petals, and stamens. Prickly pear's blossoms are typically 2–3 inches wide. Its leaves are brown and deciduous.

Range: Minnesota to Massachusetts, south to Florida and Oklahoma.

CARROT FAMILY **Umbelliferae**

QUEEN ANNE'S LACE
Daucus carota

A lacy compound umbel of creamy-white flowers forms a cluster 3–5 inches wide, with a single reddish-purple flower in the center and triple-forked bracts whorled below. The cluster is slightly convex in its early days, but forms a "bird's nest" shape with age. The hairy stem supports alternate, finely divided, fern-like leaves, 2–8 inches long.

Although considered a nuisance in some areas, Queen Anne's lace once served as ornamental lace on the apparel of members of the royal court of Queen Anne and King James I. *Daucus carota* is the ancestor of the common carrot.

During wet weather, the stem below each flower cluster becomes soft and flexible, allowing the head to bend over and protect the pollen from raindrops. Plants that have lost their pollen remain upright.

Range: Throughout most of North America.

36 30 24 18 12 6 0

CATTAIL FAMILY **Typhaceae**

COMMON CATTAIL
Typha latifolia

A yellowish spike of male flowers extends above a cylindrical, extremely dense cluster of brown female flowers, which in turn crowns a tall, stiff stem. The male flowers wilt and drop off soon after shedding their pollen. Individual flowers are tiny and nearly indistinguishable, their corollas composed only of tightly packed bristles. The basal leaves are linear, blunt, and longer than the stem.

Dense colonies form by creeping rootstocks, creating excellent cover for marsh birds and muskrats. The starchy roots were dried and ground into meal by Native Americans, who also used the long, flexible leaves in house construction and wove them into mats. The downy seeds were used as pillow stuffing and insulation by colonists. The common name arises because the floral cluster resembles the erect tail of a startled cat.

Range: Throughout most of North America.

12 10 8 6 4 2 0

BACHELOR'S BUTTON
Centaurea cyanus

"Brilliant blue" is the best phrase to describe the fluffy flower head of bachelor's button; even the species name means "blue." The terminal, 1½ inch head is made up of only tubular disk flowers, although those around the perimeter are larger and simulate rays. Its grooved stem is covered with cottony, gray hair, as are the alternate, linear leaves with entire margins.

In England, single women once wore bachelor's button as a sign that they were eligible to marry.

Range: Throughout most of North America.

BLACK-EYED SUSAN
Rudbeckia hirta

This bright, cheery bloom is the state flower of Maryland. Native to the midwest, it invaded the east when it was accidentally shipped with clover seeds and planted in fields. It has since been introduced to many places in the west. This plant thrives in dry soil because of its extensive root system, and because the hairs on the leaves reduce airflow across their surfaces, reducing water loss.

A ½ inch dome of chocolate-colored disk flowers is encircled by 10–20 sterile, golden-yellow ray flowers. The stem sports bristly hairs, and the alternate, lance-shaped leaves measure 2–7 inches long. The upper leaf margins are typically toothed, while those of the lower leaves are entire.

Range: Throughout most of North America.

CHICORY
Chicorum intybus

Sky-blue flower
heads of chicory
are composed solely of ray flowers,
square-tipped, with five teeth at the end.
Stem leaves are alternate, lance-shaped,
and entire, and clasp a stiff, branched
stem. The basal leaves are coarsely
toothed and strongly resemble those
of dandelions.

Each flower head lasts only one day, but
they bloom sequentially so that a few on
each plant are always in bloom over an
extended period. The large, deep taproot
is commonly roasted and ground up for
use as a coffee substitute or additive.

Range: Throughout most of
North America.

BULL THISTLE
Cirsium vulgare

Solitary flower
heads measuring
1½–2½ inches across crown tall, *very*
prickly stems lined with alternate, spiny
leaves that are deeply, pinnately lobed
characterize this plant. Pink disk flowers
burst forth from the top of a spiny, vase-
shaped involucre of bracts.

The thistle is the national emblem of the
Scots, dating from the Danish invasion of
Scotland. Legend has it that, as Danish
soldiers were sneaking barefoot across a
pasture to surprise the sleeping Scots, one
of them stepped on a thistle and cried
out, thus warning the Scots. From this
arose the superstition that wearing a
thistle gives protection from danger.

Range: Throughout temperate
North America.

DAISY FAMILY   Compositae

COMMON DANDELION
Taraxacum officinale

The bane of homeowners everywhere, dandelions were actually cultivated as a vegetable before lawns became fashionable. The same deep taproot which makes them extremely difficult to eradicate was also roasted, ground, and used as a coffee substitute during World War II.

The common name is a corruption of the French phrase meaning "tooth of the lion," referring to the deeply toothed leaves, which grow in a dense, basal rosette that keeps competitors at a distance. These leaves, gathered early in spring when they are the sweetest, may be eaten raw in salads or boiled like spinach. The fluffy seed heads tempt children of any age. Who among us does not have fond memories of blowing off all the parachute-like seeds with one gigantic puff and watching them float lazily away?

The solitary yellow flower heads are composed only of five-lobed ray flowers. Hollow stems exude a milky juice when broken. Long, pointed bracts grow under the head, with the outer ones reflexed.

DAISY FAMILY   Compositae

COMMON SUNFLOWER
Helianthus annuus

The state flower of Kansas, common sunflower is a significant species for wildlife and humans alike. It is an important food source for many species, a staple item at most bird feeders. American Indians used the ground seeds for bread flour, the oil for cooking, mixing paints, and dressing their hair. They also extracted yellow dye from the flowers and blue dye from the seeds for use in their basketry and weaving. The generic name is derived from *helios*, the Greek for "sun." Both this and the common name originated from the fact that the flower heads rotate to follow the sun throughout the day.

Each plant may have one or several terminal heads measuring 3–6 inches across and composed of brown disk flowers and yellow, overlapping, sterile ray flowers. The alternate leaves are egg-shaped and toothed, and are covered with stiff hairs to slow air flow across the surface and reduce water loss.

Range: Throughout most of North America.

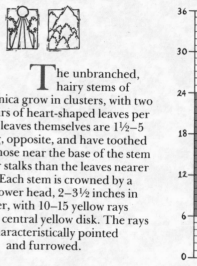

HEARTLEAF ARNICA
Arnica cordifolia

The unbranched, hairy stems of heartleaf arnica grow in clusters, with two or three pairs of heart-shaped leaves per stem. The leaves themselves are 1½–5 inches long, opposite, and have toothed margins. Those near the base of the stem have longer stalks than the leaves nearer the top. Each stem is crowned by a solitary flower head, 2–3½ inches in diameter, with 10–15 yellow rays encircling a central yellow disk. The rays are characteristically pointed and furrowed.

This western species is brilliantly showy and easy to grow in wildflower gardens from seed or a small section of rhizome. In the wild it is especially common under quaking aspens and lodgepole pines.

Range: Alaska to California, east to the Rocky Mountains.

DAISY FLEABANE
Erigeron annuus

Densely packed, fine ray flowers resemble the beard of an old man, which explains of its generic name. The white, pale pink, or pale blue ray flowers on a ½ inch head are short relative to the central yellow disk, helping to distinguish it from another common species, Philadelphia daisy. The egg-shaped, toothed leaves are 3–5 inches long and are alternate on a hairy stem.

"Bane" comes from the Anglo-Saxon word *bana*, which means "destroyer." Daisy fleabane was dried and burned in fumigating pots by pioneers to rid their dwellings of fleas and other insects. It was also used as a mattress stuffing. It was superstitiously thought to predict the sex of an unborn baby when planted, producing pink flowers if it was a girl and blue-tinged flowers if it was a boy.

Range: North America east of the Rocky Mountains.

DAISY FAMILY — Compositae

INDIAN BLANKET
Gaillardia aristata

These cheery pinwheels of color decorate much of the northern Great Plains with their large red and yellow flower heads. A similar species, *Gaillardia pulchellum*, is common along roadsides throughout the desert southwest. The solitary heads, 3–4 inches across, are composed of a red dome of disk flowers and numerous, overlapping three-toothed yellow rays with dark red or purple bases. The hairy, clasping leaves are alternate on the stem and oblong or linear in shape, often with paired lobes.

The bright colors and patterns of Indian blanket suggest those of its namesake. The generic name was given in honor of Gaillard de Marentonneau, French magistrate and patron of botany.

Range: British Columbia to Manitoba, south to Colarado and Oregon.

DAISY FAMILY — Compositae

JERUSALEM ARTICHOKE
Helianthus tuberosus

The tuber of Jerusalem artichoke, once cultivated by American Indians, is highly nutritious; it contains no starch, but consists of a form of carbohydrate that is easily metabolized by the body into simple sugars. The Lewis and Clark expedition (1805) reportedly dined on these tubers, prepared by Sacajawea, their female Indian guide, in the area now known as North Dakota. The common name is a corruption of *girasole*, the Italian for "turning to the sun," a description of the flower heads' daily movement with the sun.

There are 10–20 yellow ray flowers encompassing the central yellow disk. The thick, egg-shaped leaves are 4–10 inches long, coarsely toothed and rough in texture. They occur opposite each other on the hairy stem.

Range: East from the Rocky Mountains in North America.

MULE'S EARS
Wyethia amplexicaulis

There are 13–21 lemon-yellow ray flowers encircling the tubular yellow disk flowers on the flower heads of mule's ears. The leafy stems grow in clumps, terminating with several flower heads 3–5 inches in diameter. The middle head is usually the largest. Aromatic leaves clasp the stem alternately. They are lance-shaped with entire or toothed margins, and reach a length of 16 inches.

The generic name was bestowed in honor of Captain Nathaniel J. Wyeth, who led the botanical expedition that discovered this plant in the 1830s. The common name originated because of the long leaves' resemblance to the ears of a mule.

Range: Central Washington to western Montana, south to northwestern Colorado and northern Nevada.

MEADOW GOLDENROD
Solidago canadensis

Meadow goldenrod produces tiny, bright yellow flower heads on arching branches that form a terminal cluster. The alternate, lance-shaped leaves, 3–5 inches in length, are covered with fine hair and have *three prominent veins.*

Goldenrod is the state flower of Alabama, Kentucky, and Nebraska. It is often found growing among purple asters, and since they are color opposites, this association may make both look brighter and more appealing to the pollinating insects upon which they depend. Each colony of goldenrods is actually composed of genetic clones that originated from a single plant and spread by underground rhizomes.

Goldenrod's reputation for causing allergies is quite undeserved. Whereas goldenrod produces heavy, sticky pollen and is insect-pollinated, the real culprit is ragweed, an inconspicuous plant blooming at the same time, which is air-pollinated and responsible for many cases of hayfever.

Range: Throughout most of North America.

ORANGE HAWKWEED
Hieracium aurantiacum

Green bracts with black glandular hairs encircle the base of the flower head, which is ½–1 inch in diameter and composed entirely of orange ray flowers. Each ray has five teeth on its tip. Both the basal leaves and the stem are hairy. The leaves are 2–5 inches long, elliptical, and entire.

Orange hawkweed is often found in large colonies which make it even more conspicuous to insect pollinators. It was once believed that hawks ate this plant to improve their vision. This superstition may have began when someone observed a hawk landing in a patch of hawkweed, but never saw the mouse or vole that was the target of its attack.

Range: Minnesota to Newfoundland, south to North Carolina and Iowa.

36
30
24
18
12
6
0

OXEYE DAISY
Chrysanthemum leucanthemum

The name "daisy" comes from an Anglo-Saxon term, *daeges eye*, meaning "day's eye." It was so named because its flower heads close at night and open only during the day. Oxeye daisies were believed to ward off lightning, and so were often hung inside homes. In England, this plant is sometimes known as bruisewort because of the ability of its crushed leaves to soothe bruised skin. The stems and flowers may be dried and boiled to make a solution that soothed chapped hands.

Oxeye daisy flower heads include 15–30 broad, white rays encircling yellow, tubular flowers in a central disk with a *distinctly depressed center*. Leaves are alternate, 3–6 inches in length, and have very coarse teeth or deep pinnate lobes.

Range: Throughout most of North America.

36
30
24
18
12
6
0

PEARLY EVERLASTING
Anaphalis margaritacea

An involucre of pearly, petal-like bracts surrounds the small yellow disk of tubular flowers. Each head is ¼ inch wide and lacks ray flowers. The beauty of many flower heads is enhanced by their arrangement in a corymb, and the bracts persist long after the flowers have wilted. Long, linear leaves with wooly undersides are spaced alternately on a cottony stem. Male and female flowers are borne on separate plants; male flower heads can be identified by the yellow tuft in the center.

Range: Throughout most of North America except in the southeast.

PHILADELPHIA DAISY
Erigeron philadelphicus

Also known as Philadelphia fleabane, this species has much in common with daisy fleabane. Its fringe of white or pink ray flowers surrounding the central yellow disk was said to resemble an old man's beard, which earned it the generic name from the Greek root of the same meaning. Alternate, lance-shaped, toothed leaves clasp the stem; both leaves and stem are covered with soft hair.

As with Daisy fleabane, this plant was reputed to rid dwellings of fleas. Dried leaves and stems were burned in a pot as a fumigant, and juice from the plant was applied to the body for the same purpose.

Range: Throughout most of North America.

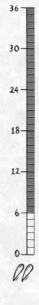

DAISY FAMILY　　　　　　　　Compositae

PRAIRIE BLAZING STAR
Liatris pychnostachya

Willowy lavender spikes of prairie blazing star swaying in the wind is a common sight on Great Plains of the United States. The species name is derived from the Greek term meaning "crowded," which describes the flower heads tightly packed in a cylindrical spike that measures up to 18 inches tall. Each head is ½ inch wide and is composed of 5–7 disk flowers, with long, purple-tipped bracts reflexed underneath. The stem is covered with coarse hair and is very leafy. Leaves are alternate, linear, and hairy. They are 4–12 inches in length with entire margins.

Range: Minnesota to Indiana, south to Louisiana and eastern Texas.

DAISY FAMILY　　　　　　　　Compositae

SPOTTED JOE-PYE WEED
Eupatorium maculatum

These flower heads are clustered in a cyme atop a tall, heavily spotted stem. They consist of disk flowers only, and are less than ½ inch wide. The entire cluster may be 4–6 inches wide. Lance-shaped leaves, 3–8 inches long and coarsely toothed, occur in whorls of 3–5.

Folklore has it that in late eighteenth-century New England, an American Indian named Joe Pye showed colonists how to use this plant to relieve symptoms of typhoid fever.

British Columbia to Newfoundland, south to North Carolina, New Mexico, and Arizona.

PERIWINKLE
Vinca minor

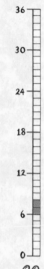

The solitary, purplish-blue flowers grow from the leaf axils of this trailing plant. A white star in the center of five spreading lobes distinguishes the tubular corolla. The flowers are about one inch wide across the lobes. Dark green, shiny, opposite leaves, 1½ inches long, make this a very attractive ground cover for wild gardens.

Periwinkle is a corruption of the Latin word *pervinca*, which means "to bind." This alludes to the creeping stem which forms dense, tangled masses.

Range: Throughout most of North America.

YARROW
Achillea millefolium

Yarrow was valued as a medicinal plant by both American Indians and pioneers. Perhaps the most useful of yarrow's properties was the stoppage of bleeding by a salve made from its ground-up, boiled leaves. Indians also used it to soothe bruises, sore throats, earaches, and burns, while pioneers found it effective at settling an upset stomach, and regulating menstrual flow.

Yarrow leaves are aromatic, especially when crushed, finely dissected and fern-like. They are arranged alternately along the stem, which is topped by a cluster of ¼ inch flower heads containing from 4–6 triple-toothed ray flowers surrounding miniscule disk flowers. At first glance yarrow resembles Queen Anne's lace, but its flower heads are arranged in a corymb, not in compound umbels.

Range: Throughout most of North America

DOGWOOD FAMILY Cornaceae

BUNCHBERRY
Cornus canadensis

Believe it or not, this small herbaceous plant is actually a close relative of the flowering dogwood tree, which may reach a height of 30 feet! It forms dense colonies by creeping rhizomes, and makes an excellent ground cover for a woodland garden.

At first glance, bunchberry seems to have a rather large flower for the size of the plant, but what appear to be large white petals are, in fact, four petal-like bracts surrounding a small globular cluster of greenish-yellow flowers, each of which consists of four petals, four sepals, four stamens, and one pistil. There are 3–9 egg-shaped leaves whorled about the stem. The leaves are 1½–3 inches long with entire margins and veins that arc from the base of the midrib to the leaf tip.

Range: Alaska to Labrador, south to Maryland, Illinois, and Minnesota.

EVENING PRIMROSE FAMILY Onagraceae

COMMON EVENING PRIMROSE
Oenother biennis

Flowers of the common evening primrose open in the evening to be pollinated by night-flying insects and close by noon the next day. This plant forms colonies of genetically identical clones via a creeping underground stem. Its seeds are often used as bird feed.

The lemon-scented flowers of common evening primrose have four shallowly-notched petals, four reflexed sepals, eight stamens, and one pistil with a cross-shaped stigma. Its leaves are 4–8 inches long, fine-toothed, lance-shaped, alternate, and hairy. The stem is also hairy and purplish in color.

Range: British Columbia south to Arizona, east to the Atlantic Ocean.

WILD BLUE FLAX
Linum perenne

These sky-blue flowers are produced in loose clusters. Each measures ¾–1½ inches wide and includes five broad overlapping petals with dark blue veins, five stamens, and five styles longer than the stamens. The alternate leaves are small and linear, angled upward, with only one vein.

Some American Indian tribes used wild blue flax to make rope and twine. This is the genus from which linen is produced, that has clothed people for thousands of years. Flax seed capsules have been found in an Egyptian tomb dating to 3,100BC, no doubt placed there to assure the deceased a supply of thread in his next life. Linen is made by soaking the stems in water until the soft tissue is rotted away. The remaining fiber is then treated to make it soft and pliant. Common blue flax, *Linum usitatissimum*, is also the origin of linseed oil as well as linen fabric. Imported from Europe for commercial purposes, it escaped cultivation and is now found in most of North America. Range: Alaska to Manitoba, south to Texas and California.

EVENING PRIMROSE FAMILY   Onagraceae

FIREWEED
Epilobium angustifolium

This is an early successional species that thrives in disturbed areas, especially following a fire. Along with other colonizing plants, it helps to stabilize soil that would otherwise be quickly eroded. American Indians used the tough fiber of the stems to make twine and fish nets.

The magenta flowers of fireweed grow in a raceme, each about an inch wide with four spreading petals, eight stamens, and a four-part stigma. Its alternate leaves are generally less than eight inches long, linear or lance-shaped, and have either a fine-toothed or an entire margin.

Range: Throughout most of North America, except in the southeast.

FORGET-ME-NOT FAMILY　　　**Boraginaceae**

TRUE FORGET-ME-NOT
Myosotis scorpioides

Forget-me-nots develop in one-sided, tightly coiled racemes that unwind as the buds bloom. The coiled raceme resembles a scorpion's tail, explaining the origin of the specific name. The doctrine of signatures dictated that forget-me-nots should be effective in treating the stings of scorpions and bites of spiders which, alas, they are not. This European import is the state flower of Alaska.

The sky-blue flowers are only ¼ inch wide. They have a five-lobed, tubular corolla with a yellow center. The leaves, measuring 1–2 inches in length, are alternate, hairy, and oblong with entire margins.

Range: Alaska to Labrador, south to Florida and Texas.

GENTIAN FAMILY　　　**Gentianaceae**

BOTTLE GENTIAN
Gentiana andrewsii

These dark blue, bottle-shaped flowers, nearly closed at the tip, form dense terminal groups and also cluster in the leaf axils. They are 1–1½ inches long, and the five stamens inside have fused anthers. The clasping egg-shaped or lance-shaped leaves have entire margins and are opposite or whorled below flower clusters.

This is one of the most common gentians, and is easily cultivated in a wildflower garden. Despite the impenetrable appearance of its blooms, pollinating insects are able to force their way inside with little trouble.

Range: southern Manitoba to southern Ontario, south to Georgia and Arkansas.

GERANIUM FAMILY   Geraniaceae

WILD GERANIUM
Geranium maculatum

Loose terminal clusters of 2–5 five pink or lavender-coloured blooms may be found on wild geraniums. Individual flowers are 1–1½ inches wide and consist of five pointed sepals, five rounded petals, ten stamens, and one pistil. The dark green basal leaves are 4–5 inches wide and have five deep, coarsely-toothed lobes.

Geranium comes from the Greek root *geranos*, which means "crane," which is suggested by the bill-shaped seed capsule of this plant. The species name means "spotted," referring to the white spots that develop on the leaves as they age. American Indians found the powdered root useful in clotting blood when they were wounded, a property due in reality to the high tannin content.

Range: Manitoba to Maine, south to Georgina and Kansas.

HEATH FAMILY   Ericaceae

KINNIKINNIK
Arctostaphylos uva-ursi

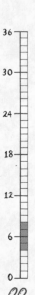

The generic and specific names of this plant both translate to "bear grape" from Greek and Latin respectively. These, plus the common name bearberry, imply that this is an important summer food source for bears of the north country, as well as for many other species of wildlife. Kinnikinnick is an Indian term for tobacco substitutes.

The height of this plant is deceptive, for it is actually a woody, trailing stem which may reach ten feet in length. Dark green, leathery leaves, oval with entire margins, are arranged alternately along the stem. The pink flowers, approximately ¼ inch in diameter, are lantern-shaped, with five lobes around the opening of the corolla.

Range: Alaska to Labrador, south to Virginia, Illinois, Minnesota, New Mexico, and California.

MOUNTAIL LAUREL
Kalmia latifolia

Mountain laurel is the state flower of Pennsylvania. In early summer this shrub blooms so profusely that it turns the entire forest understory pink, even obscuring its own foliage.

The anthers of spring-like stamens are lodged in pockets on the inside of the corolla. When dislodged by an insect, they spray pollen on its back to be transported to the nest flower the pollinator visits.

Deep pink starburst buds open into lighter pink cup-shaped corollas of five fused petals, each with two pockets and one stamen in each pocket. The evergreen leaves are alternate, shiny, and leathery. Their shape is oval or elliptical, and they are 2–4 inches in length.

Range: Indiana to Massachusetts, south to Florida and Louisiana.

PINXTER FLOWER
Rhododendron nudiflorum

Pinxter flower is a deciduous shrub which decorates the Appalachian Mountains each spring with its showy pink blossoms, characterized by five very long, upward-curving stamens and one style. The tubular, trumpet-shaped corolla has five spreading lobes. Both flowers and leaves are clustered near the ends of twigs. The leaves are 2–4 inches long, oblong, and hairy on the underside of the midrib. They are not fully developed by the time the flowers bloom, which is the reason for the species name.

Range: Ohio to Massachusetts, south to South Carolina and Tennessee.

BLUE FLAG
Iris vericolor

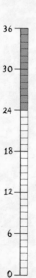

Canoeists on northern lakes are delighted by these every summer. The intricately veined purple and yellow sepals are actually functional: Such dark markings are called "bee guides" or "honey guides." They have co-evolved with insects that have learned to follow them to the nectar. On the way, the insect inadvertently pollinates the flower. The veins seem more distinct because of the contrasting background of their opposite color.

The showiest parts of this flower are actually the three drooping sepals. Three narrow erect petals seem almost insignificant by comparison. Three petal-like styles are arched over the stamens, both of which insects must squeeze under, facilitating pollination, before reaching their ultimate reward. The pale green basal leaves, 8–32 inches long, are stiff, linear, and parallel-veined.

Range: Manitoba to Nova Scotia, south to Virginia, Ohio, Wisconsin, and Minnesota.

TRUMPET HONEYSUCKLE
Lonicera sempervirens

This beautiful, high-climbing vine, which produces great quantities of nectar and a sweet scent when in bloom, is a favorite of hummingbirds, and is sure to lure them to your property should you add it to your garden.

The two-inch-long trumpet-shaped flowers, which grow in terminal whorled clusters, are scarlet outside and yellow inside with a five-lobed corolla forming two lips. Opposite, oblong, dark green leaves, 1½–3 inches in length, adorn the length of the vine. The upper pairs are fused at their bases, so that the stem appears to pierce a single leaf.

Range: Nebraska to Massachusetts, south to Florida and Texas.

COMMON BLUE-EYED GRASS

Sisyrinchium montanum

Though the leaves of this plant strongly resemble grass, the deep violet blue flower has basically the same composition of an iris; three petals, three petal-like sepals, three golden stamens, and three styles. The roundish petals and sepals are tipped with bristle-like points. The flattened stem and relatively wide leaves (¼ inch) help to distinguish this species from other blue-eyed grasses.

Sisrinchium is of Greek origin and translates to "pig snout." Wild pigs are particularly fond of the roots of this genus and have been frequently observed grubbing for them. The flowers, solitary or borne in small umbels, last only for one day, but bloom consecutively over an extended period.

Range: Manitoba to Nova Scotia, south to West Virginia and Iowa.

CANADA LILY

Lilium canadense

There are 1–20 nodding, bell-shaped blooms adorning this plant in the summer. Canada lily flowers follow the typical lily configuration of three petals, three sepals (petal-like, in this case), and six stamens. They are flecked with dark brown and vary in color from golden yellow to orange-red, although a deeper red variety does occur from Indiana to Pennsylvania southward. Lance-shaped leaves up to six inches long occur in whorls of 4–10. They have entire margins and are rough textured, even prickly, underneath.

Range: Ontario to Nova Scotia, south to Georgia and Alabama at higher elevations.

LILY FAMILY　　　　　　　　　Liliaceae

CANADA MAYFLOWER
Maianthemum canadense

Perhaps the smallest North American lily, Canada mayflower spreads by underground rhizomes to carpet large areas, making it a good ground cover for your woodland garden. It is also called wild lily of the valley.

On a small raceme grow white star-shaped flowers consisting of two petals, two sepals, and four stamens. This differs from the usual 3-3-6 pattern of most other lilies. Two clasping, heart-shaped leaves with entire margins alternate on a short stem, which zigzags at the leaf nodes.

Range: Manitoba to Labrador, south to Tennessee and Iowa.

LILY FAMILY　　　　　　　　　Liliaceae

LARGE-FLOWERED TRILLIUM
Trillium grandiflorum

The flowers of this trillium are white when the buds open, but gradually turn a medium shade of pink with age. As the common and specific names indicate, these solitary blooms are quite large (2–4 inches wide) relative to the rest of the plant. The three overlapping petals are broad, white or pink, and have an undulating margin. They flare outward from a funnel-shaped base. Three green sepals, six stamens with yellow anthers, and one pistil with a tri-lobed stigma complete each flower. There is a whorl of three broad egg-shaped or diamond-shaped leaves at the top of the stem, from which the solitary flower stalk grows. Large-flowered trilliums grow quite densely in some areas, almost obscuring the leaf litter of the forest floor.

Range: Ontario and Quebec, south to Georgia and Arkansas.

42

LILY FAMILY Liliaceae

NODDING WILD ONION
Allium cernuum

White, rose- or lavender-coloured flowers in a nodding umbel on a leafless stem characterize this species. Upon inspection, each flower is found to have three petals and three sepals. The basal leaves are linear and soft in texture, measuring 4–16 inches in length.

Nodding wild onion was one of the foods most relished by American Indians, who barbecued the bulbs in underground steaming pits to flavor other food or just by themselves. Indians introduced western explorers to wild onions as food and also as a cure for scurvy. Early French explorer La Salle supposedly marked the Algonquin Indian name for this plant, *chigagou*, on a map of the southwestern shore of Lake Michigan. The settlement that grew into a city on that spot is today named Chicago.

Range: Throughout most of North America.

LILY FAMILY Liliaceae

PURPLE TRILLIUM
Trillium erectum

A foul odor emanating from the rich burgundy-colored blossom of the purple trillium gave this woodland wildflower a most undignified name, stinking Benjamin. Its scent is similar to that of rancid meat and attracts carrion flies which pollinate the plant. Due to its smell and color, the doctrine of signatures dictated that this plant should be useful in treating gangrene; alas, it was not effective.

Six stamens with yellow anthers contrast nicely with the 1–2 inch maroon flower, composed of three petals and three green sepals. It can be distinguished from toad trillium (*T. sessile*) and prairie trillium (*T. recurvatum*) by its flower stalk and by its lack of mottled leaves and erect petals.

Range: Ontario to Nova Scotia, south to Georgia and Tennessee.

LILY FAMILY   Liliaceae

QUEEN'S CUP
Clintonia uniflora

Three petals and three sepals, all white and lance-shaped, curve outward from six stamens with yellow anthers. The solitary flower crowns a stem growing from between 2–3 shiny basal leaves, elliptical in shape and 2½–6 inches long. The fruit is a single shiny berry.

The generic name was bestowed in honor of DeWitt Clinton, former governor of New York and well known botanist of his time. Western Indians toasted the berries and leaves of queen's cup and used this concoction to make a poultice to treat cuts and eye soreness.

Range: Alaska to northern California, east to western Montana and Alberta.

LILY FAMILY   Liliaceae

SEGO LILY
Calochortus nuttallii

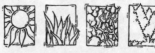

Sego lily is the state flower of Utah. The Ute Indians taught Mormon homesteaders to eat the bulbs of this lily during times of famine. The generic name comes from Greek roots meaning "beautiful grass."

Sego lily's white, bell-shaped flowers are solitary or grow in an umbel atop an unbranched stem. They are 1–2 inches wide with three broad, fan-shaped petals, three sepals, and six stamens. The petals are tinged with yellow or red above the circular glands at their base. Leaves of the sego lily are 2–4 inches long, basal, and linear, with their edges curled inward to form a trough.

Range: Montana to North Dakota, south to New Mexico and Arizona.

LILY FAMILY　　　　　Liliaceae

SMOOTH SOLOMON'S SEAL
Polygonatum biflorum

Greenish-yellow, bell-shaped flowers dangle in pairs (hence the species name *biflorum*) beneath a gracefully arching stem which is jointed, producing a zigzag effect. Alternate pale green leaves, lance-shaped and downy underneath, clasp the stem at each joint. The flowers are ½ inch long with the three-petal, three-sepal, and six-stamen composition typical of the lily family.

The circular scars on the jointed rhizome of Solomon's seal, caused by the shedding of the previous year's growth, are said to resemble the royal seal of King Solomon of 10th century BC Israel, giving rise to its common name. Each stem scar represents one year of growth, enabling the curious botanist to determine the plant's age.

Range: Nebraska to southern Ontario, south to Florida and Texas.

LILY FAMILY　　　　　Liliaceae

TURK'S CAP LILY
Lilium superbum

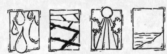

The nodding orange flower of this largest and showiest of the native North American lilies looks very much like the headgear worn by the early Turks. It flowers profusely for a lily; up to 40 of these large blooms have been observed on a single plant! The bulbs of this and other eastern lilies were dug by Native Americans for food.

Brown spots cover the strongly recurved petals and identical sepals. Six long, decorative stamens flare outward from underneath the convergence of petals and sepals. Lance-shaped leaves 2–6 inches long are alternate or whorled on the stem.

Range: New York to southern New England, south to Georgia and Alabama.

PURPLE LOOSESTRIFE
Lythrum salicaria

Purple loosestrife, a European introduction, is beautiful and aggressive. It quickly invades any wet or moist area and crowds out native wetland plants beneficial to waterfowl and other wildlife.

The flowers, a very pleasing shade of magenta, grow in long terminal spikes. They are ½–¾ inch wide, with 4–6 wrinkled petals and one or two stamens per petal. Leaves may be opposite or whorled, lance-shaped or linear, and vary from 1½–4 inches long. The leaves lower on the stem are downy and clasping.

Range: Ontario to Newfoundland, south to North Carolina and Missouri.

COMMON MALLOW
Malva neglecta

Common mallow is a low, trailing plant, and the height in this case is actually the length of its creeping stem. Its flowers, ½–¾ inch wide, grow in the leaf axils. They are radially symmetrical, with five pale lavender-colored petals notched at the tip and the stamens fused into a column around the style. The dark green, alternate leaves are round and umbrella-shaped with prominent veins and 5–7 toothed lobes. Common mallow is also known as cheeses, because its round, flat fruit resembles a wheel of cheese.

Range: Throughout most of North America.

MILKWEED FAMILY   Asclepiadaceae

COMMON MILKWEED
Asclepias syriaca

Though it is often considered a nuisance, milkweed is the soul food source of the monarch butterfly larvae and is important for this reason. Glycosides in the plant's milky juice make both the larvae and adult monarchs poisonous to predators, most of which have learned to avoid them. Another butterfly, the viceroy, has evolved to mimic the monarch, and the offspring that bear the closest resemblance to monarchs are also avoided by predators. The toxic glycosides in milkweed are quite similar to digitalins used to treat some types of heart disease. The genus was named for Aesculpaius, Greek god of medicine, because many of its members have been used to treat illnesses.

Half-inch wide regular flowers are placed in large terminal umbels. They consist of five reflexed petals, a five-lobed crown with each lobe composed of a hood and a curved horn, and five stamens. The light green leaves are opposite and oblong with entire margins, measuring 4–10 inches.

Range: Saskatchewan to New Brunswick, south to Georgia and Kansas.

MILKWEED FAMILY   Asclepiadaceae

BUTTERFLY WEED
Asclepias tuberosa

Following the unique flower structure of the milkweed family, butterfly weed blooms are regular and composed of five reflexed petals and five scoop-like structures forming a central crown. A small horn arches inward from each of these. The bright orange flowers are arranged in a large umbel. Unlike most other members of this family, its juice is not milky. The alternate leaves are linear, hairy underneath, and have entire margins. They are generally 1–5 inches long.

As the name suggests, this is a popular plant with butterflies and many other insects. Because of the precise pollination mechanism involved, fewer than one in a hundred flowers mature into fruit. Those that do, however, compensate for this by producing abundant seeds in each pod.

Early settlers chewed the tuberous root as a cure for pleurisy. They also thought that the downy seeds made a fine feather substitute in mattresses and cushions.

Range: Ontario to Newfoundland, south to Florida and Arizona

MINT FAMILY   Labiatae

CATNIP
Nepeta cataria

Catnip contains a natural insect repellent, nepeta lactone, and would be useful to protect garden plants if not for its invitation to neighborhood cats to frolic there.

Catnip flowers are purple-spotted white or pale lavender-colored, growing in short spikes atop a square stem which is covered with gray downy hair. The ½ inch tubular corolla splits into a two-lobed, hood-shaped upper lip and a three-lobed, scoop-shaped lower lip. Leaves are opposite, triangular in shape, and coarsely toothed.

Range: Throughout most of North America.

MILKWORT FAMILY   Polygalaceae

FRINGED POLYGALA
Polygala paucifolia

The magenta flowers and dark green leaves of this plant emerge from a creeping underground stem. Two of the five sepals are wing-like or ear-like, and the three petals form a tube with a delicately fringed pink or yellow crest on the lowest petal. The flowers are approximately ¾ inch long and grow in the axils of alternate, oval leaves which are about 1–1½ inches long and clustered on the upper stems.

Another name for this species is gaywings, undoubtedly bestowed because of its cheerful, perky appearance. Members of the milkwort family were once thought to increase milk production when fed to cattle.

Range: Manitoba to New Brunswick, south to Georgia, Tennessee, and northern Illinois.

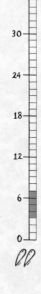

MINT FAMILY   Labiatae

OSWEGO TEA
Monarda didyma

Another name for this plant, bee balm, is a misnomer. Because of the shape of the flower and the relatively heavy weight of the bee, it is impossible for bees to pollinate it. The blossoms are a favorite of hummingbirds who can hover before them and feed at their leisure. The Oswego Indians of New York and the area's early settlers used the leaves of this plant to brew tea, hence the name.

Reddish bracts lie immediately under a dense, head-like cluster of bright red, tubular flowers. Each flower is 1½ inches long, with two stamens projecting from between an upper and a lower lip. The leaves are 3–6 inches long, opposite, egg-shaped or lance-shaped, and coarsely toothed.

Range: Michigan to New York, south to Georgia and Tennessee.

MINT FAMILY   Labiatae

SCARLET SAGE
Salvia coccinea

Scarlet sage prefers the warm coastal areas of southeastern United States. Its blooms develop on a spike of widely spaced, tiered whorls of 6–10 flowers each. The one-inch irregular flowers are bright scarlet, with a tubular, two-lipped corolla surrounded by a purple calyx. The upper lip is double-lobed, and the lower lip triple-lobed with the middle lobe notched. A scalloped margin decorates the opposite, heart-shaped leaves which average two inches in length.

Range: coastal Texas to coastal South California, south through Florida.

MINT FAMILY　　　　　　　　Labiatae

SELFHEAL
Prunella vulgaris

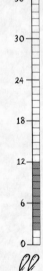

A variety of selfheal adapted to lawns blooms when only two inches tall, thereby escaping the wrath of the lawnmower. The common names selfheal and heal-all came about due to its use in treating a wide variety of throat ailments. The flower openings resemble a mouth and throat, and, according to the doctrine of signatures, that was surely what they were meant to treat, using a mouthwash made from the early spring leaves. It was also reportedly effective at stopping the flow of blood from a wound.

The ½ inch purple flowers occur in dense cylindrical spikes; the upper lip of the tubular corolla is hood-like, and the lower lip is fringed and drooping. Each bloom has four stamens inside and green, hairy bracts at its base. Lance-shaped or egg-shaped leaves, 1–3 inches long with entire margins, grow opposite each other on a stem square in cross-section.

Range: Throughout most of North America.

MINT FAMILY　　　　　　　　Labiatae

WILD BERGAMOT
Monarda fistulosa

This aromatic herb is actually named after an unrelated European citrus fruit with a similar fragrance. The leaves are commonly used in making mint tea, and oil from the leaves was once used to treat respiratory ailments, possibly dictated by the doctrine of signatures due to the flower's resemblance to a gaping mouth and throat.

A circular cluster of inch-long lavender flowers caps the square, hairy, branched stems of wild bergamot. The tubular corollas consist of a hairy two-lobed upper lip and a broad three-lobed lower lip. Two stamens project from the opening. Its leaves are opposite, lance-shaped, coarsely toothed, and may be as much as 2½ inches long.

Range: southern British Columbia to southern Quebec, south to Georgia and Arizona.

FIELD BINDWEED
Convolvulus arvensis

Field bindweed's name describes its habitat and the tendency of the twining stem to "bind" anything in its path. The scientific name, from the Latin roots *convolvo*, meaning "entwine," and *arvensis*, meaning "of cultivated fields," is similarly descriptive. Thus, simply knowing the name tells us what to look for and where to look for it. This low, creeping vine is extremely hardy and aggressive. Its deep roots make it especially difficult to eradicate. Other members of this family are cultivated, however; some, for their showy flowers, and the sweet potato for its edible tubers.

The flowers are one inch wide, their five petals fused into a white or pink trumpet-shaped corolla which encircles five stamens. Field bindweed's leaves are rather small, ¾–1½ inches long, alternate, and triangular with entire margins.

Range: Throughout most of North America.

WILD MINT
Mentha arvensis

 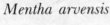

The strongly aromatic leaves announce the presence of this plant even if the rather inconspicuous flowers do not. The glands of wild mint yield oils that are distilled to make peppermint and spearmint flavorings for the food industry.

Quarter-inch flowers are whorled in the leaf axils. Their pale lavender-colored or white four-lobed corollas with four protruding stamens are dwarfed by two-inch opposite leaves. The leaves are egg-shaped or lance-shaped with toothed margins.

Range: Throughout most of North America.

MUSTARD FAMILY   Cruciferae

DESERT PLUME
Stanleya pinnata

T his large, brightly colored wildflower of the arid western states is particularly noticeable against the gray sagebrush among which it often grows. Its presence indicates that the soil in which it grows contains selenium, a toxic mineral. Therefore, the use of soils that once supported desert plume is avoided in strip mine reclamation.

Willowy racemes of luminous yellow flowers crown the tall, blue-green, leafy stems of desert plume. Four long, linear petals covered with dense hair on the inner surfaces near their base constitute the corolla, and four yellow sepals, the calyx. There are both basal and alternate bluish-green leaves, 2–6 inches long, with narrow pinnate lobes.

Range: Southeastern Oregon to western North Dakota, south to western Texas and southern California.

12 10 8 6 4 2 0

MUSTARD FAMILY   Cruciferae

BLACK MUSTARD
Brassica nigra

Y ellow, cross- shaped flowers grow in narrow racemes on the ends of widely branched stems. The ½ inch wide, regular corollas each have four petals and four sepals. Leaves on the lower portion of the stem are deeply lobed, having four or more lateral lobes and one larger terminal lobe, while the upper leaves are lance-shaped. All leaves are alternate.

Black mustard seeds are used to make pickles and table mustard, two condiments familiar to nearly every American. Other members of this genus include such important garden vegetables as broccoli, cauliflower, Brussel sprouts, turnips, rutabaga, kohlrabi, and cabbage.

Range: Throughout most of North America.

36 30 24 18 12 6 0

NIGHTSHADE FAMILY　　Solanaceae

BITTERSWEET
NIGHTSHADE
Solanum dulcamara

Violet, star-shaped flowers grow in loose, drooping clusters along the climbing stem of this plant. Five pointed, reflexed lobes encircle a brilliant yellow cone of fused anthers extending well beyond each ½ inch-wide corolla.

Portions of the plant, if eaten, taste first bitter, then sweet. It is toxic but usually not lethal for humans, and in fact its fruit, a bright red berry, is a source of food for some wildlife. Bittersweet nightshade was used in England at one time to counteract witchcraft. Ironically, it was also used by the witches themselves to make a poisonous brew.

Range: Throughout most of North America, rare in arid regions.

NIGHTSHADE FAMILY　　Solanaceae

JIMSONWEED
Datura stramonium

Jimsonweed is very poisonous and hallucinogenic. American Indians took small doses of the plant to facilitate "visions" that would help them unravel the mysteries of the universe. The common name is a corruption of "Jamestown weed," so named because it poisoned many British soldiers sent to Jamestown, Virginia, to quell Bacon's Rebellion in 1676. After running low on supplies and eating the spiny fruit of Jimsonweed, they, too, had "visions."

Five white or violet petals are united into a wavy, funnel-shaped corolla, 3–4 inches long. A tubular green calyx extends nearly half the length of the corolla. Jimsonweed leaves are 2–8 inches long, alternate, egg-shaped, and coarsely toothed.

Range: Throughout most of North America.

PINK LADY'S SLIPPER
Cypripedium acaule

This orchid is also known as the moccasin flower. It grows primarily in the dry, acid soils common in pine and oak forests.

The lip of the solitary flower is heavily veined, with a deep fissure forming a hollow pouch. Large oval leaves, covered with silver hair underneath, grow from the base of the plant, while the downy stem is leafless. The bloom's color ranges from deep rose to pastel pink, and a white variety is found at the northern limits of its range.

Lady's slipper blooms are well engineered for their purpose. Once a bumblebee, its primary pollinator, enters the pouch, exit by the same route is prevented by the inwardly-curled edges. Nectar-coated hairs entice the bee upward toward two special exit holes near the top of the sac. In order to escape through either hole, the bee must make contact with the modified stigma, a bright green pad positioned so as to scrape off any pollen on the bee's back that was acquired from previous flowers. A small projection at each exit innoculates the bee's back with more pollen to be transported on to the next lady's slipper. Thus, the species ensures its cross-pollination.

Range: Saskatchewan to Newfoundland, south to Georgia and Alabama.

DOWNY RATTLESNAKE PLANTAIN
Goodyera pubescens

Downy rattlesnake plantain's small white flowers are arranged in a dense cylindrical spike atop a fuzzy stem. They are somewhat globe-shaped, with the upper sepal and two lateral petals forming a hood over the cupped lip petal. Broad, white-veined leaves are grouped in a rosette at the base of the plant.

The pattern on the leaves resembles a rattlesnake's back, which points to its use as a snakebite remedy. Leaf litter often hides the bold pattern of its leaves, making it less conspicuous. Though not a true plantain, it was so named because of its basal rosette leaf configuration, which is similar to the plantains.

Range: Ontario to Quebec, south to Florida and Arkansas.

ORCHID FAMILY   Orchidaceae

YELLOW-FRINGED ORCHID
Habernaria ciliaris

This strikingly beautiful, orangish orchid, with its drooping, long-fringed lip petal, blooms in a large spike. Its upper sepal and two lateral petals are erect, the lateral sepals are spreading, and a 1½ inch spur projects downward and backward from the lip petal. The leaves are 3–10 inches long, alternate, and lance-shaped.

A close relative, the purple-fringe orchid, uses a method of cross-pollination that is presumably similar in the yellow-fringed orchid. Pollen masses, each bearing a sticky disk that protrudes below the anther, attach to the tongue of a moth as it attempts to reach nectar in the spur. The moth unwittingly carries the pollen mass on to next yellow-fringed orchid to begin the plants life cycle anew.

Range: Wisconsin to New York, south to Florida and eastern Texas.

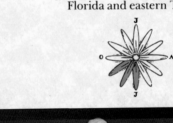

ORCHID FAMILY   Orchidaceae

ROSE POGONIA
Pogonia ophioglossoides

Lateral pink petals arching over a fringed, yellow-bearded lip distinguish rose pogonia from a similar orchid, grass pink, whose yellow-fringed lip occurs at the top of the flower.

One or occasionally two terminal flowers perch on top of the stem with a leaf-like bract growing beneath each. A single lance-shaped leaf clasps the middle of the stem. Rose pogonia requires the acid soils of wet meadows, sphagnum bogs, and wetland margins.

Range: Ontario to Newfoundland, south to Florida and Texas.

LEADPLANT
Amorpha canescens

A characteristic shrub of upland prairies, leadplant's common name comes from its gray appearance. The pinnately compound leaves, consisting of 15–45 leaflets, are covered with dense, woolly gray hair, and the stem is likewise hairy. Its tiny purplish-blue flowers have only one petal, the standard, and ten bright orange stamens.

With its very deep taproot, leadplant is ideally suited for competition with prairie grasses, whose roots intercept much of the precipitation near the soil surface. The taproot also helps leadplant survive the periodic fires necessary to maintain a prairie ecosystem. Indians used the woolly leaves of this plant as a tobacco substitute and to brew tea.

Range: Southern Saskatchewan to Michigan, south to Arkansas and New Mexico.

GROUNDNUT
Apios americana

Sweetly scented maroon racemes arise from the leaf axils of this climbing vine. The keel of each ½ inch flower is scythe-shaped and upturned. The leaves are 4–8 inches long and pinnately compound with 5–7 lance-shaped leaflets.

American Indians gathered the root, an edible tuber, and the Pilgrims, during their first years in the New World, depended on this as one of their staple foods. They reportedly used it in soups and stews, and fried them like potatoes.

Range: Minnesota to Nova Scotia, south to Florida and Texas.

PEA FAMILY   Leguminosae

RED CLOVER
Trifolium pratense

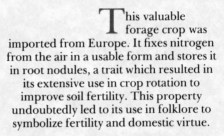

This valuable forage crop was imported from Europe. It fixes nitrogen from the air in a usable form and stores it in root nodules, a trait which resulted in its extensive use in crop rotation to improve soil fertility. This property undoubtedly led to its use in folklore to symbolize fertility and domestic virtue.

Varying from pink to magenta, the flowers grow in dense, round, terminal clusters. The alternate, compound leaves are palmately divided into three fine-toothed, hairy leaflets, each marked with a light chevron.

Red clover, the state flower of Vermont, is pollinated exclusively by bumblebees, which are perfectly proportioned by size and weight for this task. The pollen is located at the base of the flower, whose opening is just large enough to accomodate the bee's head. As it struggles, the bee triggers the pistil, which springs up to collect the pollen of previously visited flowers from its head. Next, the stamens spring up, dusting the bee's head with their own pollen. So dependent is red clover on bumblebees that when it was imported to Australia as forage for sheep, it would not regenerate until bumblebees were also imported.

Range: Throughout most of North America.

PEA FAMILY   Leguminosae

PRAIRIE FALSE INDIGO
Baptisia leucantha

Whitish flowers with a very characteristic pea shape are borne on stiffly erect, foot-long racemes. The common name indicates the content of a deep blue pigment, becoming visible as the bushy plant dries, that resembles indigo, a dye derived from a tropical member of the pea family. Alternate leaves are palmately divided into three oblong segments, each 1–3 inches long.

Range: Ontario, south to Mississippi and Texas.

PICKERELWEED
Pontederia cordata

The funnel-shaped flowers of this aquatic species are less than ½ inch long. A tubular corolla, split into upper and lower lips, surrounds six stamens, three long and three short. Two yellow spots adorn the larger middle lobe of the upper lip. The glossy, dark green basal leaves are heart-shaped, 4–10 inches long, and extend above the water's surface.

Pickerelweed is found in shallow, quiet water. It has established its niche between cattails and loosestrife, which grow closer to shore, and water lilies and water hyacinths, which prefer deeper water. Its leaf stalks are composed of loosely arranged cells with many air spaces in between, allowing air to reach the submerged parts of the plant. Pickerel, the predator fish for which this plant is named, stalk the shallows or lie in ambush amongst pickerelweed or other shallow water vegetation.

Range: Ontario to Nova Scotia, south to Florida and Oklahoma.

WILD BLUE PHLOX
Phlox divaricata

Light blue and slightly fragrant, these flowers grow in a panicle at the top of a sticky stem with creeping shoots at its base. The five spreading lobes, sometimes notched at the tip, narrow dramatically at their bases, where they fuse to form a long, slender tube. The opposite, clasping leaves, 1–2 inches long, are egg-shaped or lance-shaped with entire margins.

The common and generic names have their origins in the Greek word meaning "flame," a reference to the brightness, not necessarily the color, of the flowers in certain members of this genus. The sweet scent of wild blue phlox, also known as wild sweet William, is especially strong in the early evening.

Range: Minnesota to Quebec, south to South Carolina and eastern Texas.

PICKERELWEED FAMILY   Pontederiaceae

WATER HYACINTH
Eichornia crassipes

Spikes of showy, lavender, funnel-shaped flowers of water hyacinth emerge from the quiet shallows of southern waters. The six-lobed flowers, the uppermost lobe being larger with a conspicuous yellow spot, include six stamens and average two inches in width. Shiny, bright green leaves are supported by "floats," inflated sacs of spongy, air-filled tissue on the leaf stalks. They are 1–5 inches wide and round or kidney-shaped with entire margins.

Water hyacinths were introduced from the tropics and have spread rapidly, clogging waterways and generally making a nuisance of themselves. They do have at least one redeeming quality aside from their attractive blooms; their lush growth may help remove excess nutrients in the water which result from fertilizer washing into ponds and streams from agricultural land. This condition could otherwise result in explosions of algae populations which deplete dissolved oxygen in the water and sometimes result in massive fish kills.

Range: Missouri to Virginia, south to Florida and Texas, also in southern California

PINK FAMILY   Caryophyllaceae

BOUNCING BET
Saponaria officinalis

Bouncing bet's sweetly scented white or pink flowers are produced in dense terminal clusters on leafy, unbranched stems which are swollen at the leaf nodes. The base of the flower is encased in a tubular calyx with five teeth around its tip. Five broad petals, notched at their tips, are reflexed, exposing ten stamens and two styles. The opposite leaves are oval or lance-shaped, 1½ inches long, with entire margins and 3–5 prominent veins.

Thick sap, containing saponins which produce lather when mixed with water, is responsible for the generic name, derived from the Latin root *sapon*, which means "soap." Colonial housewives planted bouncing bet in their gardens for use as an alternative to lye soap. It was also found effective in cleaning and lightly bleaching fabric, and was once planted near textile mills for this purpose.

Range: Throughout most of North America.

PITCHER PLANT
Sarracenia purpurea

Pitcher plant's leaves are perhaps even more noteworthy than its unusual flower. This plant has adapted to nutrient-poor habitats such as bogs, where decomposition, the breakdown of plant and animal tissue, is extraordinarily slow. In order to acquire the nutrients it needs, particularly nitrogen, pitcher plants have utilized an unlikely source: insects!

A basal rosette of leaves are inflated into hollow, upward-curving green pitcher shapes veined with red. The inside of the pitchers are covered with stiff, downward-pointing bristles, preventing the escape of the insects who crawl in to investigate. Eventually, they fall into water collected at the bottom of the pitcher and drown. Enzymes secreted by the plant, along with naturally-present bacteria, then digest the meal.

Purplish-brown flowers, approximately two inches wide, crown tall, slender, leafless stalks. They are composed of five broad petals, numerous stamens and a pistil with a style expanded into a large, umbrella-like cap.

Range: Saskatchewan to Labrador, south to Florida and Texas.

DEPTFORD PINK
Dianthus armeria

The base of this blossom is enclosed in a long, tubular calyx having five pointed lobes. Five toothed petals, deep pink and dotted with white, form a bilaterally symmetrical corolla ½ inch wide. The stiff stem is swollen at the nodes of opposite, linear leaves, which are 1–2 inches long.

Deptford pink was once common in fields near Deptford, now an industrial section of London, England. It is a close relative of the carnation, *Dianthus caryopyllus*, commonly sold by florists.

Range: Ontario to Nova Scotia, south to Georgia and Missouri; also Washington and Oregon, east to Montana.

POPPY FAMILY **Papaveraceae**

CALIFORNIA POPPY
Eschscholzia californica

California's state flower, the California poppy, grows so profusely within its range that the spring and summer blooms often turn entire hillsides orange. The flowers close at night and on cloudy days, a rarity in the southwest. They often intermingle with miniature lupins, whose violet blooms serve to make the orange poppies appear brighter, and vice versa, because they are color opposites. Native Americans cooked and ate the leaves of California poppy, and used the juice of its roots as an anesthetic.

The solitary blooms are colored various shades of golden-orange and deep orange, with a distinct pink rim around the base of the ovary. They are normally 1–2 inches wide, composed of four fan-shaped petals and many stamens. Their spicy fragrance attracts pollinating beetles. The fern-like leaves are less than three inches long and highly divided into many segments.

Range: Southern Washington through California, east through southern Arizona and southern New Mexico.

POPPY FAMILY **Papaveraceae**

BLOODROOT
Sanguinaria canadensis

Numerous golden-orange stamens surrounding a single pistil distinguish this otherwise white woodland wildflower. Eight to ten petals complete the solitary, 1½ inch wide bloom. The basal, palmately lobed leaves are 4–8 inches wide, and will curl around the base of the plant to conserve warmth on cool spring nights.

Bloodroot's name comes from the red-orange juice of its roots. American Indians used this juice as a dye for baskets, clothing, war paint, and also as an insect repellent and a cure for coughs and colds. *Sanguinaria* originated from a Latin term that means "bleeding."

Range: Manitoba to Maine, south to Florida and eastern Texas.

FRINGED LOOSESTRIFE
Lysimachia ciliata

Fringed loosestrife's yellow, star-shaped flowers, ¾ inch wide, are displayed on slender, arched stalks arising from the leaf axils. Each regular flower includes five round, finely toothed petals with sharp points at their tips, and ten stamens attached to the petal bases. Curiously, five of the stamens are sterile. The opposite leaves range from 2½–5 inches in length, and are fringed with stiff hairs on their stalks. They are egg-shaped or lance-shaped with entire margins.

This genus is named for Lysimachus, a 3rd century BC Macedonian general, who was credited with "loosing strife" on the battlefield when he found that these plants quieted troublesome beasts of burden.

Range: Washington to Nova Scotia, south to Georgia and Arizona.

DUTCHMAN'S BREECHES
Dicentra cucullaria

This is a favorite woodland find and a popular addition to wildflower gardens. The flowers bear a humorous resemblance to a pair of old-fashioned pantaloons hung out to dry. Its primary pollinator is the bumblebee, one of the few insects with a proboscis, the insect equivalent of a tongue, long enough to reach the nectar stored in the spurs. Honeybees are able to reach the pollen, but not the nectar, so there is less incentive for them to visit Dutchman's breeches.

The unique shape of this fragrant white flower is due to the outer two of its four petals, which are inflated into two nectar-containing spurs. It's generic name, in fact, is a descriptive Greek term meaning "two-spurred." Together, they form a "V" shape with a yellow opening at the bottom. Several flowers are strung along a leafless stem, which sometimes arches over to give the illusion of a clothesline. The basal, compound leaves are grayish-green and have a feathery appearance.

Range: North Dakota to Nova Scotia, south to Georgia and Arkansas; also in Washington, Oregon, and Idaho.

PURSLANE FAMILY **Portulacaceae**

PURSLANE
Portulaca oleracea

These small yellow flowers occur either singly or in small clusters in the leaf axils or at the end of the stem. Each has two sepals, five petals, and eight or more stamens. The stem is a succulent, shiny, bronze, prostrate creeper that may reach 24 inches. On it, succulent, spoon-shaped leaves are arranged alternately.

Purslane is renowned for its tenacity; even if pulled out by the roots, it continues to live on stored food and water until its seeds mature. It was brought to North America from Asia as a medicinal plant. The generic name originated from *portula*, meaning "little gate," because of the lid on the seed capsule.

Range: Throughout most of North America.

PRIMROSE FAMILY **Primulaceae**

STARFLOWER
Trientalis borealis

The sight of this delicate woodland nymph is quite a contrast next to the mighty giants of its timbered habitat. Two white, starburst flowers arise on long, thread-like stalks from a single whorl of 5–9 shiny green leaves. The blossoms are ½ an inch wide and normally consist of seven petals and seven stamens with yellow anthers. Whorled at the top of the stem, the leaves are 2–4 inches long and lance-shaped with entire margins.

Trientalis is a Latin word meaning "one-third of a foot," which is indicative of the plant's height.

Range: Saskatchewan to Labrador, south to Virginia and Illinois.

PURSLANE FAMILY   Portulacaceae

SPRING BEAUTY
Claytonia virginica

W hite or pink petals striped with deep pink form bowl-shaped flowers which grow in loose racemes. Each flower is ½–¾ inch wide and includes two sepals, five petals, and five stamens with pink anthers. Dark green, linear leaves, 2–8 inches long, usually occur in a single, opposite pair midway up the stem.

Spring beauties are among the earliest spring wildflowers, their blooms disappearing as the forest canopy leafs out. Although small, the flowers are impressive in large patches. They last only three days, opening on sunny days and closing at night and on overcast days. The underground tubers have a sweet chestnut flavor and were gathered as food by both Native Americans and the early colonists.

Range: Ontario to Quebec, south to Georgia and eastern Texas.

ROSE FAMILY   Rosaceae

DWARF CINQUEFOIL
Potentilla canadensis

Y ellow flowers, ½ inch wide with five petals and numerous stamens and pistils, stand on long stalks attached to the leaf axils near ground level. The palmately compound leaves are each composed of five oval leaflets which may grow to 1½ inches in length. Dwarf cinquefoil's leaflets are toothed only on the outer half of their margin, while the half nearest the base remains entire. This helps to distinguish it from another similar species, common cinquefoil, whose leaflets are toothed all the way around the margin.

Dwarf cinquefoil is an indicator of nutrient-poor soil, for it will grow where many other species will not. In folklore it symbolizes maternal love, for, during rain, the leaves reportedly bend over to cover the flowers, as a mother would protect her child. Witches allegedly used cinquefoil as a drug, inducing a trance-like state by rubbing it on their bodies. Oddly, cinquefoil was also believed to be an effective protection against witches.

Range: Ontario to Nova Scotia, south to Georgia and Missouri

ROSE FAMILY   Rosaceae

WILD STRAWBERRY
Fragaria virginiana

Who among us does not have fond childhood memories of finding the season's first sweet wild strawberries ripening in a sunny area near our home? Though small and difficult to pick in quantity, the effort is well worth the trouble, for their taste is arguably superior to their cultivated relatives.

The strawberry connoisseur should begin in mid-spring to look for the ¾ inch-wide white and yellow flowers in order to locate the best crops. The blooms consist of five round white petals surrounding numerous stamens and pistils attached to a yellow dome-like structure, the receptacle, which enlarges to become a juicy red strawberry after fertilization. The individual seeds are embedded in pits on the berry's surface. Wild strawberry leaves have long-stalked, palmately compound leaves with only three toothed leaflets. Like many other members of its family, this species commonly spreads by runners.

Range: Throughout most of North America.

ROSE FAMILY   Rosaceae

SHRUBBY CINQUEFOIL
Potentilla fruticosa

This small shrub is characterized by reddish-brown, shredding bark on its twigs. The one-inch wide yellow flowers, possessing five petals and numerous stamens and pistils, are produced singly in the leaf axils and in clusters at the ends of branches. Its leaves are pinnately compound, divided into five oblong, hairy leaflets, each less than one inch long with entire margins.

Fruticosa, the specific name, means "shrubby." Shrubby cinquefoil is an indicator plant to both ranchers and wildlife biologists. It is not a preferred food of cattle or deer, so when it is grazed to the point where the plant is stunted or killed, that shows that the population of animals in the area is higher than that habitat can support.

Range: Alaska to Labrador, south to Pennsylvania and California.

SAXIFRAGE FAMILY   Saxifragaceae

FOAMFLOWER
Tiarella cordifolia

The protruding stamens and spreading petals of these small white flowers in terminal racemes impart a feathery appearance to the flower clusters. Each flower is ¼ inch wide and comprised of five sepals, five white petals, two pistils, and ten stamens with reddish or yellow anthers. Bearing a resemblance in shape to maple leaves, those of foamflower are 2–4 inches long, basal, lobed, coarsely toothed, and hairy.

Foamflower spreads by underground rhizomes to form dense colonies which make an excellent ground cover in shady wooded sites. The delicate texture of such a mass of flowers gives the appearance of foam, for which it is named.

Range: Ontario to Nova Scotia, south to North Carolina and Tennessee.

ROSE FAMILY   Rosaceae

WOODS ROSE
Rosa woodsii

Saucer-shaped blooms of woods rose are formed by five broad, overlapping petals which encircle numerous yellow stamens. These sweet-scented flowers vary in color from deep pink to white, and are born on thorny branching stems. The bluish-green leaves are pinnately compound with 5–7 oval, coarsely toothed leaflets each approximately one inch long.

Wild roses, which typically have only 5–7 petals, are the ancestors of the elegant garden roses so prized by gardeners around the world. They have undergone centuries of intense hybridization to yield varieties that today produce massive blossoms with hundreds of delicate petals in different colors.

Range: British Columbia to Ontario, south to Missouri and California.

BUTTER-AND-EGGS
Linaria vulgaris

Such a perky wildflower as butter-and-eggs seems somehow out of place in the waste soils of its preferred habitats, but it nevertheless brightens North American roadsides, railroad beds, and other disturbed areas throughout the summer. Five fused petals constitute the irregular corolla, forming a two-lobed upper lip and a three-lobed lower lip with a prominent nectar-filled spur at its base. Four stamens, five sepals and a pistil complete the flower. The alternate leaves are linear and grow to 1½ inches in length.

Butter-and-eggs flowers are equipped with orange "honey guides," which direct insects to the nectar while they simultaneously pollinate the flower. Many flowers possess such markings, and their effectiveness has been clearly demonstrated. Experiments have shown that as hummingbird moths try to stick their proboscis into butter-and-eggs blossoms pressed between glass, the marks they leave on the glass strongly coincide with the location of the honey guide; clearly these, and probably most other pollinating insects, know exactly where to look for nectar, which increases the likelihood of pollination occurring.

Range: Throughout most of
North America.

COMMON MULLEIN
Verbascum thapsus

Flowers of common mullein grow in long, dense spikes. Five yellow petals are fused to form a tubular corolla with five spreading lobes, which encloses five stamens and one pistil. The leaves of this species are particularly noteworthy for their soft, woolly texture. They are oval or egg-shaped, 4–16 inches long, and occur in basal rosettes, alternately on the unbranched stem.

The common name comes from the Latin root *mollis*, which means soft. Another common name is Quaker rouge. When rubbed on the skin, the barbed hairs on the leaves of common mullein irritate it, causing a redness to appear. While Quaker religion dictates that its members may not use cosmetics, the women of this denomination discovered that the use of this plant allowed them to enhance their appearance without violating the rules of their faith.

Range: Throughout most of
North America.

INDIAN PAINTBRUSH
Castilleja coccinea

The inconspicuous flowers of this species are actually hidden in the axils of scarlet-tipped, fan-shaped bracts that may be mistaken for blossoms. The flowers are one inch long, greenish yellow tubular corollas with a long two-lobed upper lip arched over a three-lobed lower lip. Elliptical leaves, 1–3 inches long with entire margins, are produced at the base of the plant, while those on the stem are alternate and divided into narrow lobes.

The red-tipped bracts appear to have been dipped in paint: According to legend, an Indian trying to paint a picture of a sunset grew frustrated at his inability to capture the vibrant colors. He asked the Great Spirit for help, who gave him brushes dipped in the colors of the sunset, and where these were discarded a colorful plant grew.

Range: Southern Manitoba to New Hampshire, south to Florida and Oklahoma.

ELEPHANT HEADS
Pedicularis groenlandica

These little wonders bear an amazing resemblance to their namesake. The long outer upper lip of this pink flower curves forward beyond the lower lip to form the "trunk." The outer two lobes of the lower lip become the "ears," while the middle lobe completes this miniature pachyderm replica. They bloom in dense racemes on at leafy stem, with the alternate leaves pinnately divided into toothed lobes. The leaves are 2–10 inches long.

Elephant heads are pollinated exclusively by bumblebees. They bloom just as worker bumblebees emerge in the spring. Their rapid wingbeats dislodge clouds of pollen which the bees then collect.

Range: Alaska to Alberta, south in the mountains to California and New Mexico; also in northern Ontario, Quebec, and Labrador.

SNAPDRAGON FAMILY **Scrophulariaceae**

TOWERING LOUSEWORT
Pedicularis bracteosa

This species produces yellow, purple, or maroon flowers in a dense terminal raceme. The irregular blossoms are less than one inch long, and the upper, two-lobed lip of the corolla arches downward over the lower lip like a hawk's bill. The fern-like leaves, 3–10 inches long, are pinnately compound, divided into many narrow, coarsely toothed leaflets.

Pediculus, the Latin root from which the generic name originated, means "little louse." It was assigned due to the mistaken belief that livestock would suffer lice infestation if they ate these plants.

Range: British Columbia to Alberta, south to Colorado and northern California.

SNAPDRAGON FAMILY **Scrophulariaceae**

TURTLEHEAD
Chelone glabra

These bilaterally symmetrical blooms are usually creamy-white, but may also be pink or greenish-yellow, and they are sometimes tinted with a lavender color. The upper lip arches over a hairy lower lip, enclosing five stamens inside the corolla, one of which is short and sterile. Toothed, lance-shaped leaves, 3–6 six inches long, are located opposite each other on the stem.

The generic name is Greek for "tortoise," and the blossoms do indeed simulate the head of these familiar reptiles. Bumblebees and honeybees pollinate turtlehead, sometimes disappearing entirely inside the flower in the quest for nectar.

Range: Ontario to Nova Scotia, south to Georgia and Missouri.

ROUND-LEAVED SUNDEW
Drosera rotundifolia

In this case, the leaves of the plant are more noteworthy than the flower. Sundews are insectivorous plants, able to thrive in nutrient-poor soils because of their ability to catch and digest insects. The round leaves, for which this species is named, are covered with bristly hairs each tipped with a jewel-like drop of clear sticky fluid. Insects that alight on the leaves become ensnared, and the hairs then fold inward to the surface of the leaf where digestion takes place via secreted enzymes. In 1875, Charles Darwin discovered that these hairs respond when touched with a bit of meat or animal hair, but, interestingly, they did not repond to inorganic objects such as bits of gravel!

Despite their vital function, round-leaved sundew flowers are rather inconspicuous. They are white or pink, barely ¼ of an inch across, and possess five petals. They are produced on small, one-sided racemes, but open only one or two at a time in sunlight.

Range: Throughout most of North America; absent in arid western regions.

ASIATIC DAYFLOWER
Commelina communis

Two round, blue petals above and one small white petal below comprise the corolla of this ½ inch-wide flower, which grows singly or in small clusters. Three sepals and six stamens with yellow anthers are also included in each blossom. The lance-shaped leaves, 3–5 inches long, clasp the stem alternately.

Flowers bloom for only one day. It forms colonies by rooting from the leaf nodes of its creeping stem, hence the specific name *communis*, "in a group." The generic name symbolizes three Dutch brothers named Commelin, two of which became well-known botanists (the two blue petals) while the third did not (the small white petal).

Range: Wisconsin to Massachusetts, south to Alabama and Arkansas.

TEASEL
Dipsacus sylvestris

In a truly unique floral arrangement, the purple blooms of teasel are borne on an egg-shaped spike, usually 2–4 inches long, with spiny bracts protruding between the flowers and, most notably, long spiny bracts curving upward from the base of the spike. The flowers, ½ inch long with a tubular corolla, begin blooming in the middle of the spike and progress upward and downward in two purple bands. Leaves are lance-shaped, toothed and opposite, measuring 4–16 inches long. The upper pairs of leaves are fused at their bases.

Teasel's common name comes from the old practice of wool maufacturers, who placed the dried flower heads on spindles to "tease" the wool. It is popular in dried floral arrangements.

Range: Throughout most of North America; absent in the desert southwest.

SPOTTED TOUCH-ME-NOT
Impatiens capensis

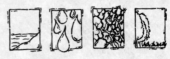

Also known as jewelweed for the manner in which raindrops bead up on the leaves and shine like crystalline jewels, spotted touch-me-not is well-known to children. They delight in detonating the spring-loaded, ripened seed pods, which explode at the slightest touch, propelling their seeds many feet away from the parent plant. The juice of the stem and leaves is effective in relieving the itching caused by poison ivy. American Indians also used it to treat athletes foot and other skin ailments, for it does indeed contain fungicidal chemicals.

Golden-orange flowers spotted with reddish-brown dangle horizontally from the leaf axils by drooping stalks attached near the mouths of the corollas. The inch-long, funnel-shaped flowers are composed of three petals and three sepals, one of which is the same color as the petals and forms a pouch with a nectar-filled spur. The stem is succulent and translucent, and the leaves are pale green, egg-shaped, and less than four inches in length.

Range: Alaska to Newfoundland, south to Florida, Texas, and Oregon.

VIOLET FAMILY Violaceae

BIRD-FOOT VIOLET
Viola pedata

Bird-foot violet is most easily identified by its fan-shaped, basal leaves, 1–2 inches long, with linear segments that somewhat resemble the toes on a bird's foot. The pale lilac-purple flowers have five beardless petals; the lower petal is nearly white with purple veins, a central groove, and a backward projecting spur. Five stamens are made conspicuous in the throat of the flower by their orange anthers.

The number of flowers on a violet plant is an indicator of soil richness in the immediate area; the more blooms a plant produces, the better the soil quality.

Range: Southern Ontario to southern Quebec, south to Florida and Texas.

VIOLET FAMILY Violaceae

COMMON BLUE VIOLET
Viola papilionacea

One word, describes the common blue violet: *fragrant*. Their flowers are normally blue, but may be nearly white. They are irregular with five petals, the lower petal larger and spurred, the two lateral petals bearded to comb pollen from visiting insects. The basal, heart-shaped leaves may be as wide as five inches, and have a scalloped margin. Violets are the state flowers of Illinois, New Jersey, Rhode Island, and Wisconsin. Common blue violet has a fascinating back-up reproductive mechanism. If the spring flowers are not pollinated due to rainy or cold weather, it produces "blind flowers" at or below gound level. These have no petals or fragrance, do not open, and are self-pollinating. They produce large quantities of seeds which can grow into clones of the parent, ensuring the survival of its genes until better conditions prevail.

Range: Saskatchewan to Nova Scotia, south to Florida and Texas.

SWEET WHITE VIOLET
Viola blanda

These fragrant white flowers have the five petals typical of all violets, but the upper two petals of sweet white violets are *twisted and bent backward* and its flower stalks are reddish. These two traits help to distinguish them from northern white violets, which occupy much of the same range but bloom about two weeks earlier and prefer moist forests and stream banks. The heart-shaped, basal leaves are approximately 2½ inches wide, dark green, and shiny.

An interesting historical note: violets were the symbol of Bonapartists, the supporters of exiled Napoleon Bonaparte, who promised to return with the spring violets. He did.

Range: Ontario to Quebec, south to Georgia and Tennessee.

VIOLET FAMILY   **Violaceae**

DOWNY YELLOW VIOLET
Viola pubescens

The canary yellow flowers of this species decorate northeastern forest floors before the canopy leafs out later in the spring. They are ¾ inch wide with five petals, the lower three veined with dark purple and the lateral two bearded. Its hairy, heart-shaped leaves are between 2–5 inches wide, and alternate on a downy stem.

The specific name, *pubescens*, means "hairy," and refers to the stem and leaves. Dark purple veins on a field of the opposite color, yellow, serve as guides to direct insects to the nectar while they inadvertently pollinate the flower. Old-time chemists once used the juice from crushed violet leaves to detect acids and bases; acid turns the juice red, and bases turn it green.

Range: Ontario to Quebec, south to Virginia and Missouri.

WATER LILY FAMILY Nymphaceae

FRAGRANT WATER LILY
Nymphaea odorata

Though the stems of water lilies may reach four feet or more in length, their leaves only float on the water's surface and the flowers protrude barely a few inches above it. The fragrant flowers of this species, for which it is named, are 3–5 inches across and possess many white or pink petals arranged in a starburst shape. The numerous stamens in the center are bright yellow. Its round, floating leaves, up to 12 inches in diameter, have a distinct "V"-shaped notch cut into their base.

Stomata, the openings in the leaves through which respiration of gases occur, are located on the upper surface, rather than on the lower surface as is normal for terrestrial plants. The spongy stem has four air ducts for transportation of gases to the rhizomes buried in the mud. These rhizomes, incidentally, are a favorite food of muskrats; look for their lodges where you find water lilies.

Range: Throughout most of North America, most common east of the Rocky Mountains.

WATER LILY FAMILY Nymphaceae

YELLOW POND LILY
Nuphar variegatum

What look like petals are actually six showy petal-like sepals comprising the globe-shaped flower. There are numerous petals, but they are quite small and hidden from view unless one looks directly down into the bloom. A myriad of stamens surround a disk-like stamen in the middle of the flower. Yellow pond lily's round floating leaves, 3–15 inches in diameter, also have a "V"-shaped notch at their bases, but it is not as sharply angular as that of fragrant water lily.

The large floating leaves of water lilies help reduce overheating of shallow water in summer, making it habitable for cold-blooded creatures such as fish, reptiles, amphibians, and insects, whose body temperatures are controlled by their environment. The leaves also provide resting sites for small frogs, dragonflies, and even small birds.

Range: Manitoba to Quebec, south to Delaware and Nebraska.

WATER PLANTAIN FAMILY   Alismataceae

ARROWHEAD
Sagittaria latifolia

Sexes are separate in these white flowers, which occur in whorls of three on a spike composed of several whorls. Each flower has three sepals, three white petals, and numerous yellow stamens or a yellow sphere of pistils. The basal leaves, 2–16 inches long, have a very distinctive arrowhead shape.

The rhizomes of arrowhead, which is also called wapato, produce starchy, edible tubers that float to the surface when the mud is disturbed. These were called duck potatoes by early settlers; they are a favorite food of ducks and muskrats. American Indians opened muskrat lodges to raid their caches of these tubers.

Range: Throughout most of North America.

WINTERGREEN FAMILY   Pyrolaceae

INDIAN PIPE
Monotropa uniflora

Indian pipe is an unusual looking wildflower. This saprophytic plant is totally devoid of chlorophyll. Through a symbiotic relationship with a fungus, it derives all of its nourishment from decaying organic matter in the soil. The benefit to the fungus is not clear, so it might be that Indian pipe is parasitic on the fungus.

A translucent stem, covered with waxy, scaly bracts, turns suddenly downward like a shepherd's crook to support a solitary, nodding flower. The white, or sometimes salmon, flower is ½–1 inch long and consists of 4–5 petals, 10-12 stamens, and a pistil.

Range: Throughout most of North America, absent in the desert southwest.

WINTERGREEN FAMILY   Pyrolaceae

SPOTTED WINTERGREEN
Chimaphila maculata

These nodding, fragrant flowers are each composed of five white or pink waxy petals bent back to expose ten stamens and a knobby pistil. They grow in a small cluster at the top of the stem, which also supports lance-shaped evergreen leaves. These leaves are whorled on the stem, mottled with white, and have a white stripe along the midrib.

The generic name comes from two Greek roots meaning "winter loving," alluding to the evergreen nature of the leaves. The specific name, *maculatum*, is Latin for "spotted." An extract of this plant was once a common ingredient in root beer.

Range: Michigan to New Hampshire, south to Georgia and Arizona.

WINTERGREEN FAMILY   Pyrolaceae

PIPSISSEWA
Chimaphila umbellatum

These nodding pink or cream flowers develop in a corymb, each with five scoop-shaped petals bent back at their bases, curving forward at their tips to expose ten stamens attached around the base of a fat red or green ovary. The whorled leaves are dark green, lance-shaped, coarsely toothed, and have a leathery texture.

Pipsissewa comes from a Cree Indian word meaning "it breaks into small pieces." Native Americans used this plant medicinally to break up kidney stones.

Range: Alaska to Quebec, south to Georgia and California

WOOD SORREL FAMILY — Oxalidaceae

COMMON WOOD SORREL
Oxalis montana

The flowers of common wood sorrel have five white or pink petals veined with deep pink, five sepals, and ten stamens attached at the base of an ovary with five styles. They are radially symmetrical and average ¾ inch in width. The clover-like basal leaves are palmately compound with three heart-shaped leaflets.

Wood sorrel leaves have a sour taste due to their oxalic acid content. They are sometimes used to spice up salads, but are poisonous in large quantities. The generic name comes from the Greek *oxys*, "sour."

Range: Manitoba to Newfoundland, south to Pennsylvania and Ohio, and in the mountains to North Carolina and Tennessee.

WOOD SORREL FAMIL — Oxalidaceae

REDWOOD SORREL
Oxalis oregana

These radially symmetrical flowers are ½–¾ inch wide and somewhat funnel-shaped. They each have five pink or white petals with purplish veins and ten stamens attached to the base of an ovary with five styles. The basal leaves are palmately compound with three heart-shaped leaflets. Each leaflet is ½–1½ inches long with a pale spot in the center.

Redwood sorrel forms lush carpets on the floors of redwood and douglas fir forests; few other wildflowers grow so densely in these coniferous forests. Wood sorrels are easily identified by their clover-like leaves.

Range: Washington to central California.

APPENDIX

FOR MORE INFORMATION, CONTACT:

National Wildflower Research Center
2600 FM 973 North
Austin, TX 78725–4201
(512) 929–3600

FURTHER READING:

Austin, Richard. 1986. *Wild Gardening: Strategies and Procedures Using Native Plants*. New York, NY: Simon and Schuster.

Dennis, John. 1985. *The Wildlife Gardener*. New York, NY: Alfred A. Knopf, Inc.

Ernst, Ruth Shaw. 1987. *The Naturalist's Garden*. Emmaus, PA: Rodale Press.

Leighton, Phoebe and Calvin Simonds. 1987. *The New American Landscape Gardener*. Emmaus, PA: Rodale Press.

Martin, Laura. 1984. *Wildflower Folklore*. Chester, CT: Globe Pequot Press.

Paulsen, Annie (editor). 1989. *The National Wildflower Research Center's Wildflower Handbook*. Austin, TX: Texas Monthly Press.

Philips, Harry. 1985. *Growing and Propagating Wildflowers*. Chapel Hill, NC: The University of North Carolina Press.

Shaw, John. 1984. *The Nature Photographer's Complete Guide to Professional Field Techniques*. New York, NY: Watson-Guptill Publications.

Smyser, Carol. 1982. *Nature's Design*. Emmaus, PA: Rodale Press.

Ward-Harris, Joan. 1983. *More than Meets the Eye*. Toronto, Ontario: Oxford University Press (Canadian Branch).

PICTURE CREDITS

INDEX

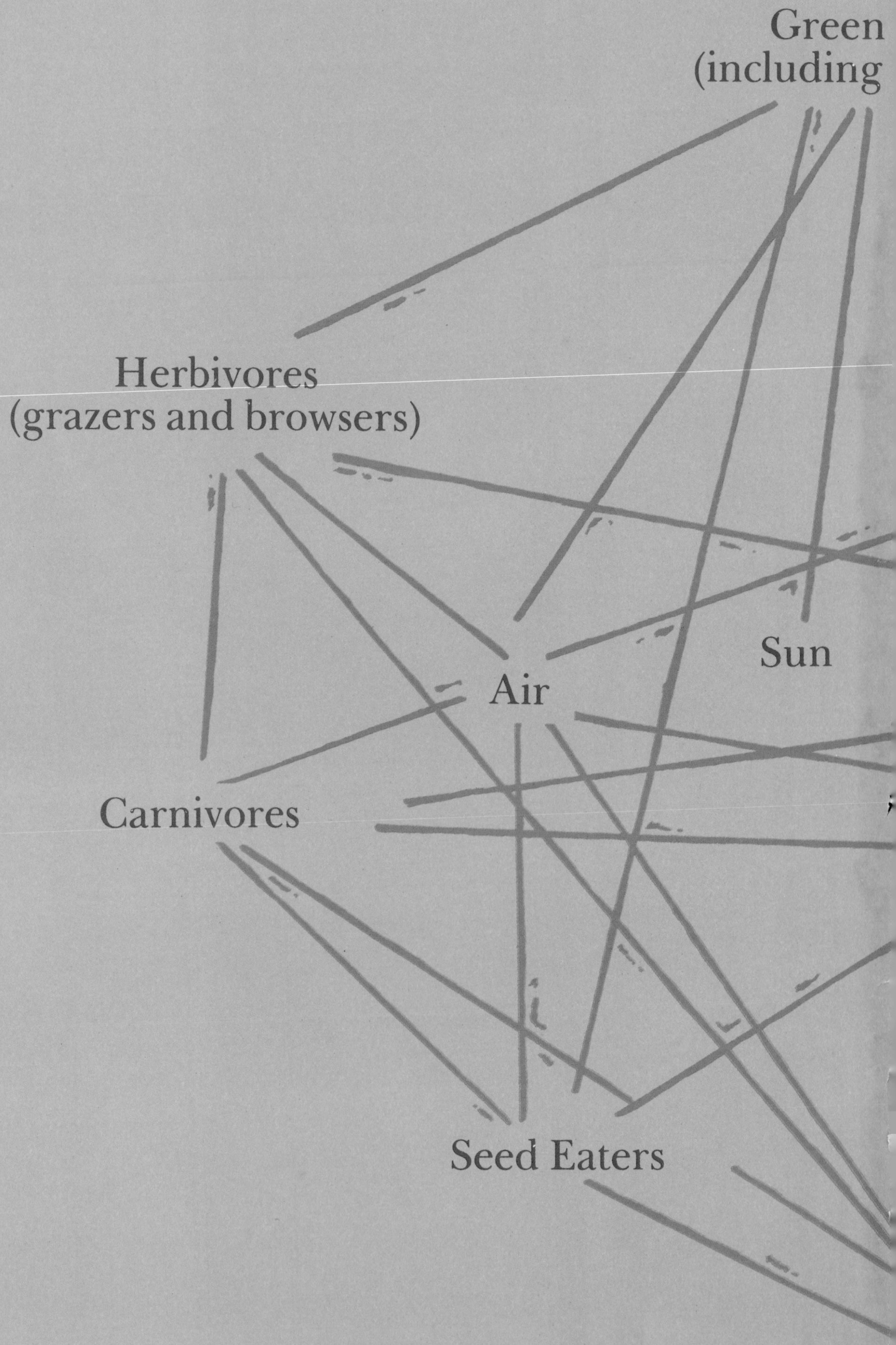

Green
(including

Herbivores
(grazers and browsers)

Sun

Air

Carnivores

Seed Eaters

(including